THE UNDERGROUND CITY
OF CAPPADOCIA

Unity and the Great Persecution

By
Edward Feuer

Copyright © MMXIV Edward Feuer

Full revision MMXXIII
Registered with the US Copyright Office

All rights reserved. No part of this book may be reproduced in any form or by any electronic or mechanical means – except in the case of brief quotations embodied in articles or reviews – without the written permission of the Author.

Cover:
Special thanks to Brent Gordon and Tamara Nunez
Modification of a painting from the Catacomb of San Callisto from the 3rd century.

I want to thank the people who stood by me through the challenges of writing this book. I could not have completed it without your help.

Dr. David Levy
Randy Ballas
Debbie Lindgren
Christina Cole
Mike Gaetke
Brew Briggs
Jim Smith
and especially my amazing mother Annette Foyer

Table of Contents

PREFACE	5
THE NEW PROJECT	13
CREATING COMMUNITY	29
GALERIUS	42
THE WAR	62
FLEE!	75
ARRIVAL	85
NEW RECRUITS	98
A NEW SUPREME EMPEROR	106
BATTLE BELOW	118
MONTH ONE: "BE ONE"	128
MONTH TWO: "COMPLETE UNITY"	141
MONTH THREE: "THERE IS ONE BODY"	157
MONTH FOUR: "KEEP THE UNITY OF THE SPIRIT"	175
MONTH FIVE: "ONE VOICE"	187
MONTH SIX: "PRECIOUS OIL"	193
MONTH SEVEN: "AGREE WITH ONE ANOTHER"	202
MONTH EIGHT: "BE OF ONE MIND"	209
MONTH NINE "LIVE IN PEACE WITH ONE ANOTHER"	213
MONTH TEN: "ONE FLOCK"	219
THE TUNNEL	224
THE VICTORY	230
THE RISE OF CONSTANTINE	240
EXTRAS	250

FINAL THOUGHTS	***259***
NOTES	***263***
ABOUT THE AUTHOR	***267***

PREFACE

Cappadocian Rocks, Murat Ozstoy CC

I first heard about Cappadocia and the underground cities when a friend returned from a trip to Turkey. He described the huge underground dwellings he had visited that were built by early Christians. I did some research and was absolutely amazed at my findings.

The ancient people of Cappadocia lived in caves forged out of the strange rocks that cover the landscape. There are still people living in these caves to this day.

Underground City of Cappadocia

Cappadocian Cave Home, Wiki CC

The first underground city was discovered in 1963 when a man was working on a closet in his cave-home. He accidentally broke through a wall and found a passageway that went deep underground. Archeologists were brought in, and they explored an intricate system of stairways that went down 21 levels! They saw a large chapel, a well, stables for animals, sleeping quarters and everything needed for survival. Each level was protected by a huge stone door. They also discovered a five-mile tunnel that led them to another city of equal size. Some archeologists estimate that these cities can occupy over 40,000 people each. Many believe that these underground cities are as great of an ancient marvel as the pyramids in Egypt.

Preface

They have discovered over 200 underground cities in Cappadocia and just recently in 2015, they uncovered the largest city to date.

Underground City Chapel, Martin Ciglar CC

Before the rise of Constantine, a questionably Christian emperor (311AD), persecution was rampant within the Roman Empire. The most intense period occurred from 303 AD to 311AD during a period known as 'The Great Persecution.' The historian Eusebius was imprisoned and tortured during the Great Persecution but lived to convey a detailed account. He estimates that over 1,000,000 people died during this time. The culprit? An evil Roman emperor named Galerius. Unknown to most people, historians refer to him as the 'Adolph Hitler' of his day.

Apparently, Christians used these underground cities to protect themselves from torture, enslavement, and death. In the 7th century, they were most likely used for protection against invading Muslims.

Underground City of Cappadocia

Underground City Diagram, Yasir999, CC

The underground cities of Cappadocia were kept secret by the early Christians. There is nothing in the history books mentioning or describing them. However, historians tell us that early church leaders traveled to Cappadocia during times of persecution. One can only assume that the early Christians were hiding in these underground cities.

To build cities of the magnitude that we see in Cappadocia, all done with utmost secrecy, the believers of that period had to share an important quality:

UNITY

The goal of a leader is to unite people for a common cause. Look at any great leader throughout history and it all comes down to unity.

Jesus is the ultimate leader, uniting us to God and to one another. In this book, I have tried to clearly contrast the two types of leadership:

THE ROMAN STYLE VS. THE CHRISTIAN STYLE

As you will see from the story, the Romans would exalt the most ruthless, selfish, cruel, and manipulative person to a position of authority. Their system is contrasted by the Christian style of leadership. In Christian leadership, the leader is chosen by God and empowered by the Holy Spirit to fulfill a calling to serve and to guide. At the heart of Christian leadership is servanthood.

Jesus directly refers to the 'Roman style' of leadership, comparing it with the 'Christian style':

> **Jesus called them together and said, "You know that the rulers of the Gentiles lord it over them, and their high officials exercise authority over them. Not so with you. Instead, whoever wants to become great among you must be your servant, and whoever wants to be first must be your slave, just as the Son of Man did not come to be served, but to serve and to give his life as a ransom for many."**
>
> **-Matthew 20:25**

It doesn't take long to figure out that many Christians function apart from the Biblical rules of engagement. When it comes to business, relationships and ministry, the scriptures are often thrown out the window as Christians often employ 'Roman' tactics. They attack others to rise to power, manipulating their way into a position of control. They will often appear as the spiritual 'alpha dogs', as they seek to become the person in charge.

The Roman characters in this story are all real and much of the dialogue was taken directly from historical records.

The Christians living down below in this story are purely fictional. However, after the Great Persecution ended, incredible Christian leaders emerged from Cappadocia. They were instrumental in bringing Christians together as a united force for a season in history.

Eusebius discusses the division between the churches just before The Great Persecution:

> "...and those whom we esteemed as our shepherds, throwing aside the bond of holiness, were excited about being in conflict with one another, and did nothing else than heap up strife and threats and jealousy and enmity and hatred toward each other."
>
> -Eusebius 325AD, History of the Church VIII, (8)

The Great Persecution was one of the most brutal times in history, and yet, the hardships were clearly instrumental in bringing unity to the body of Christ.

CS Lewis writes:

> "I could well believe that it is God's intention, since we have refused milder remedies, to compel us into unity, by persecution even and hardship. Satan is without a doubt nothing else than a hammer in the hand of a benevolent and severe God."

Jesus prays:

> "My prayer is not for them alone, I pray for those who will believe in me through their message, that all of them may be one, Father, just as you are in me and I am in you."
>
> -John 17:2

Welcome to Cappadocia.

PART ONE

"...In fact, everyone who wants to live a godly life in Christ Jesus will be persecuted. While evildoers and impostors will go from bad to worse, deceiving and being deceived."

2 Timothy 3:12

CHAPTER 1

THE NEW PROJECT

Cappadocian Home, Charlton, CC

March 1, 302AD

283 years after the Roman Empire Conquered Cappadocia

Daniel woke up with a wonderful sense of peace. Waking up had been dreadful for some time. It was as if someone was standing over him with a whip, lashing him with torturous thoughts.

The project, he thought to himself. *Today we start the project.*

He jumped out of bed, propelled by a new vibrancy. Then he glanced at his wife from the bedside, just as she opened her eyes.

Anasia had a unique look compared to all the dark-haired women of Cappadocia. Her chiseled features, blond hair and jewel-like blue eyes made it difficult not to stare at her. For Daniel, after 12 years of marriage, her poignant beauty had been overshadowed by a list of resentments. Fortunately for the two of them, the tide was turning on their relationship.

Daniel whispered to his wife, "Good morning my love."

She looked back and stared at him, surprised that he would speak to her with such affection.

Daniel said confidently, "I believe that God is going to protect us. We're going to get through all of this."

Dark storm clouds were appearing on the horizon as a brutal new emperor was rising within the Roman Empire. Since the time of Jesus, persecution intensified or decreased depending on the emperor in power.

Anasia looked into Daniel's eyes. His thickly bearded face had a piercing gaze of resolution. She hadn't seen that look on him in a long time.

He then continued as his eyes began to glisten, "You are my gift from above. I took you for granted for so long, but not anymore."

Daniel hadn't cheated on his wife, but he had contemplated leaving her. His eyes had been distracted by all the beautiful women around town, compromising his relationship.

Only because of Anasia's strong walk with God had she faithfully stood beside her husband, enduring a difficult and painful marriage. She had prayed day and night for him, that he would experience the love from God that she had known.

He leaned over and the two kissed, but then he quickly turned and began to put on his black work toga. His large head popped through the hole.

"Where are you going?"

"I'm off to meet Ozgur. Remember, today we start working on the project."

"That's right," she said as she turned to try to sleep some more.

Daniel went into the other room and recited a scripture that he was memorizing. He sat with a parchment in his hand as he repeated the verse aloud:

> "A new command I give you: Love one another.
> As I have loved you, so you must love one another.
>
> -John 13:34

Anasia celebrated this moment, for her husband had been indifferent to spiritual things throughout their marriage. Finally, God was answering her prayers. He had grown up in a Christian family and at different moments, had tried hard to live like his parents and the community around him. Recently, his spiritual life had caught fire, making all the difference in their relationship.

Daniel then put down the parchment and grabbed his bag of tools. He quickly left the house and set foot onto one of the busiest streets in Cappadocia.

Merchants were already selling their goods at the bustling market area. He walked past a bakery and caught a whiff of the freshly baked bread. Right next to the bakery was a shop where they sold slow roasted lamb. In the early morning, customers anxiously lined up because they usually sold out in the first hour. Everybody was talking about a new spice that made the succulent lamb even more delicious.

Cappadocia was a major trading post, featuring exotic foods and desirable merchandise from all over the world. The region was a hub along the Silk Road where traders came from as far away as China to buy and sell. Items such as exotic spices, brilliantly colored clothing, aromatic perfume, and unique pottery filled the market district.

The region's most desirable women were also drawn to the market area, but since Daniel stopped gawking at them, he saw them more as an obstacle rather than an attraction.

It was time to say goodbye to this place that was central to everything he had esteemed so dearly. He felt like a soldier, going off to war and possibly to never return.

He walked past a cave home that he helped to construct several years before. This was one of his favorite projects. The owners were out front, waving at Daniel.

The landscape of Cappadocia is covered with mystical rock towers and cones. Some of these naturally occurring rock structures are perfectly cylindrical, reaching over 130 feet high and are unlike anything on the planet.

The Cappadocians chiseled through these rocks and transformed them into indestructible cave homes. Many people migrated to the area, just to live in one of these incredible rock houses.

Daniel was a master craftsman with a hammer and chisel. Throughout his life, he loved doing one thing, creating homes for people. He worked harder than anyone else, and his incredible passion led to a great reputation as a master home builder.

Unfortunately for Daniel, he recently lost his home in a bad business deal to a Christian named Gilley. He and his wife were forced to move in with his uncle. The recent loss of their home put added pressure on a marriage that was already struggling.

The turning point for Daniel happened two months ago when a man named Nicolas befriended him. Nicolas was an astute businessman, raising horses for a living. He was also very well versed in the scriptures. He saw that Daniel was struggling and so he started meeting with him once a week. Nicolas would simply listen to Daniel's problems and then pray with him. He also asked Daniel to start memorizing certain scriptures. Nicolas became like a father to Daniel.

Daniel experienced transformation just by praying with a strong believer and memorizing the Bible. Eventually, Nicolas asked Daniel to start praying with his wife. Each night before bed, the couple prayed with each other. Dramatically, things really started to turn around for the better.

Daniel's uncle gave him some property in a rural area, far away from the city where he grew up. The couple decided to move and develop an underground Christian community with friends. After this decision, Daniel and his wife both experienced a deeper sense of peace and a surge of inner strength. Despite all the turmoil, they knew that they were headed in the right direction.

Daniel walked past his old house, the one he recently lost. He had grown up in this home before it was swindled away from him by Gilley. Many of his most cherished memories were bundled up in this house. He stopped for a second to take a glance when a familiar sound hit him like a rock to the head. It could be heard all over the Roman Empire:

Cracking whips followed by screams of agony.

After turning a corner, he was met by a group of Roman soldiers standing guard over about 100 slaves. Someone told Daniel that the Romans started branding the faces of their slaves. Out of curiosity, he stopped to see if it was true. Normally, he tried to look the other way whenever he saw slaves because it was such a depressing sight, but he had a compulsion to look.

The slaves were chained at the neck, wearing tiny loincloths. Their bodies were fully exposed to the morning cold and the piercing whips of the soldiers.

When Daniel saw the mark on their faces, he could not believe his eyes. It spanned the entire forehead. These men had no hope of ever returning to a normal life. The mark read, 'Fugitive'. If a slave ran away, everyone would instantly know that this man was a slave on the run.

The soldiers randomly whipped the slaves as they grinned in sinister delight. Daniel recognized one of the slaves as someone he knew from church. He stared in shock just as the man noticed him.

One of the soldiers pointed at Daniel and yelled, "Move on!" Daniel turned his head and continued walking.

The Cappadocians dreamed of breaking away from the empire, but the Roman grip was much too strong. Whenever there was any hint of rebellion, the Romans would torture and enslave anyone that was even potentially involved, quickly squelching any uprising. Their inconceivable cruelty and complete lack of empathy gave them an unfair advantage over any adversaries. The Romans had controlled Cappadocia for close to 300 years, and it didn't look like anything was ever going to change.

Daniel saw his good friend Ozgur waiting in front of his house. He walked up and greeted him with a rugged hug. The two men looked like they were brothers with their brawny physiques, medium height, and thick beards.

Daniel said to Ozgur, "I just saw Bildau from church. I heard he had been enslaved because he supposedly owed taxes, but we all know he was apprehended because he is a believer. Pretty soon they are going to grab all of us."

"I saw him there yesterday," Replied Ozgur, "It could have been me, or it could have been you. It's just a matter of time until they grab all of us."

Daniel looked at Ozgur in the eyes and asked in a low voice, "Do you know what you're getting yourself into with this project?"

"Yes," Ozgur replied confidently.

"How do I know that you're not going to quit? I'm telling you right now that if we start, you better not quit!" demanded Daniel.

Ozgur responded, "I won't let you down. I'm not Gilley. I know what you have been through."

Daniel then turned in the direction of the slaves and asked, "What are they building?"

Ozgur replied, "A new jail, complete with a courtyard for torture and executions. Some have said that they are making more room for the Christians."

"Right next to your home," said Daniel, "I can see why you would be so eager to join us. But still, let me say it again. Don't waste my time Ozgur! If you are not going to follow through, I don't want to start!"

"If the property is as you say, I'll commit 100%," said Ozgur, with a tone of resolution that satisfied Daniel.

The two men had been childhood friends and part of the same church in Cappadocia for most of their lives. Ozgur's wife had died a few months ago, and he recently lost his job as an architect with the government. He had a senior position and was responsible for some of the most highly respected projects in Cappadocia. When Roman soldiers appeared at his work and commanded him to worship the emperor, he refused and was fired after fifteen years of faithful service. With his reputation as a celebrated architect, he thought that they would never fire him.

The two men started making their way out of town. They walked past a blockade of soldiers which always caused fear. Fortunately, they were allowed to proceed.

As they walked side by side, Ozgur asked, "You told me that you owed money for taxes and have nothing, how did you suddenly get this property?"

Daniel replied, "Anasia and I were caring for my uncle Yousef while he was dying. Yousef never married. We were his only surviving relatives, and he owned the home where we are staying right now. We thought he was going to give it to us before he passed away, but then he said he had promised it to someone else! We were crushed!

He believed that God wanted us to have the cave I'm going to show you. My uncle hid in this cave during the last wave of persecution several years ago. Like all of us, he sensed another crisis coming and wanted us to be safe. What I didn't tell you is that the cave has an indoor well."

"Are you serious Daniel?" asked Ozgur. Water was a rare commodity in Cappadocia.

"Yes," said Daniel, "My uncle lived in town, but traveled periodically to this cave to make sure nobody was trying to claim it. He always kept it ready just in case persecution picked up again. He also gave us the surrounding lands as far as the eye can see."

After walking for more than two hours and seeing nobody but a few shepherds, they approached a small unassuming cave. Daniel stopped and said with a smile, "We're home!"

"Well, I really like the area," said Ozgur, "And the best part? No Romans anywhere! Amazing Daniel!"

"Here's what I like," said Daniel, pointing to a peach tree next to the entrance. "My uncle planted this. The surrounding ground is fertile, perfect for crops."

"My favorite!" Ozgur hastily grabbed one of the plump fruits as juices gushed down his face after taking a big bite.

"This is amazing!" Ozgur exclaimed.

Daniel smiled and pulled out his lamp from his bag. Then he took out some oil and carefully poured it into the lamp. After striking a rock with a flint, he ignited a small pile of twigs. He used one of the twigs to ignite his lamp. Then he smothered the fire with some dirt and stomped on the smoldering pile.

He carefully opened the rickety old door as they stepped inside the small musty cave. Daniel pointed to a large pot and said, "A staircase is hidden underneath."

The two struggled to move the huge water pot, revealing a hole in the ground. Each man climbed into the hole and then walked down six flights of stairs. They found themselves in a large room with a hole in the floor. Daniel located a pot that was connected to a long rope. After slowly letting down the pot into the hole, they heard sloshing sounds. He pulled up the dripping pot and offered Ozgur a drink.

After Ozgur guzzled down the water, he joyfully exclaimed, "It's as pure as it gets!"

After taking some for himself, Daniel asked, "Are you in? Let's seal the deal," as he extended his hand.

Ozgur replied, "We can be safe. I don't see an alternative for us. With the well and a stockpile of food, there is no end to how long we can stay down here. I'm excited! We'll build a stable for animals. We'll make this place as good as it can be!"

"Hey, 100%. I demand a 100% commitment."

"100% commitment!" affirmed Ozgur as he shook Daniel's hand.

"Good," said Daniel. "Well, let's get started with building the church."

The two made their way back up to the third level to a small room.

When they entered, Daniel said, "This space needs to be a lot bigger."

After a quick analysis, Ozgur pointed to one of the walls and said, "Let's start by expanding over there."

Daniel pulled out his hammer and chisel. He began to attack the wall in front of him with unbridled fervor. Big chunks of rock fell to the ground as he pounded away. Although Daniel managed teams of workers, he always worked hard himself, seeking to be an example to those working with him. When workers saw his passion, they were also motivated to work hard.

The cadence of the hammer and the chisel created music that was sweet to Daniel's ears. He was working again, and his body felt alive! All the money that he made from work went to pay the unfair tax collector. There was no way he could ever pay off what was demanded, so he stopped working for the past several months.

Suddenly, Daniel's shoulder began to ache due to an old injury. Then he experienced waves of fatigue rolling over him. He tried to fight through it, but then his mind asked him, *what am I doing here? This is nonsense. Why should I work hard on a project like this? I should be making real money.*

Daniel handed Ozgur the hammer and chisel and then began to pick up the rock fragments. Bending over, he felt a sharp ache in his back. Then he climbed up the stairs to the entrance with the rocks. The reality of the amount of work that was required on this project hit him hard.

As Daniel stepped outside, his mind began to focus on Gilley.

"Fake Christian!" he exclaimed out loud as if Gilley were standing in front of him. "Disgusting swindler!"

The relationship between Gilley and Daniel had started as a noble endeavor. After meeting at church, the two men partnered to build a new inn for travelers. Gilley was to provide financing and Daniel was to manage the construction. After completion, the two were going to share in the profits. With a verbal agreement in place, Daniel worked hard for a full year. Anasia didn't trust Gilley, but Daniel ignored her warnings. Then suddenly, Gilley refused payment to him and his workers. He told Daniel that he was tired of paying for everything, and that Daniel needed to contribute his share of the cost of construction. Gilley completely changed their verbal agreement. He stated that unless Daniel contributed financially, he would take over the whole project.

Gilley said he would lend Daniel the money to pay his share if he would secure the loan with his home. Daniel had no other choice but to agree to his terms. Just after the agreement, Daniel was given a big tax bill by the local tax collector. The tax collector was bribed by Gilley. If Daniel didn't pay right away, he faced possible enslavement at the hands of the Roman Empire.

When he missed several payments on the loan, Gilley confiscated his property and took over the construction project. Daniel tried to take the matter before members of his church, but Gilley refused to meet with them. Daniel considered taking him to court, but the local judge was corrupt and one of Gilley's good friends.

Daniel saw pictures of Gilley in his mind. He spoke aloud while gritting his teeth, "You're nothing but a selfish liar! How can you call yourself a Christian?"

Daniel drifted back to the job in front of him as he dumped the rocks into the canyon. He watched the rocks explode as they hit other rocks.

Afterwards, Daniel entered the cave again as Ozgur handed him back the tools. He started pounding as hard as he could on the wall, venting his full frustration toward Gilley on the rocks. But then...

"Ahhhh!!!" screamed Daniel as the hammer smashed part of his thumb. He grabbed his hand and then said, "Let's take a break."

The two men went outside and sat down with their backs to a rock, looking out at the expansive desert terrain. Daniel considered giving up on the project as he hid his pain from Ozgur.

"Something is wrong. I can see it on your face."

Daniel did not say anything. He continued to look forward.

"I have a scripture for you Daniel,

> **"Unless the Lord builds the house, the laborers labor in vain."**
>
> **-Psalm 127:1**

Ozgur continued, "We need to ask God to build this project through us. Otherwise, we are completely wasting our time. Let's pray."

Daniel nodded his head in agreement but continued to stare forward.

Ozgur began to pray passionately about the work ahead. He said, "God, you have led us to this place. Fill us with your Spirit and please do your work through us! Please protect us from the evil Romans!"

Suddenly, a powerful supernatural peace blanketed the two men. For Daniel, the serenity lasted a few seconds as thoughts about Gilley reentered his mind. Daniel exclaimed, "I keep thinking about what Gilley did to us!"

Ozgur said, "That is Satan at work. Daniel, don't you understand? God can bless you and give you much more than what Gilley took away, but you must leave all the resentment behind. You can't follow God and have resentment. I know he hurt you. Let it go Daniel. I beg you, please, just let it go!"

"I just want to know; how does Gilley get away with it? Where is God's justice?"

Ozgur said, "Jesus commands us to count the cost of being a Christian. One of the costs is that we forgive. Trust God and don't look back. He delivers justice. If Gilley has wronged you in any way, God will correct him. He is faithful to correct you. Isn't he?"

"Definitely. I don't get away with anything," said Daniel, "However, Gilley hasn't asked me for forgiveness and therefore I don't have to forgive him! He hasn't repented."

Ozgur replied, "We must follow Jesus' example. He asked for forgiveness for those who were killing him! He said, "Father forgive them for they know not what they do." We can protect and distance ourselves from people, but we can't hold onto resentment. Harboring resentment will stop us from seeing our prayers answered, stripping our lives of God's blessing."

Daniel replied, "I've tried to forgive him, and I just can't!"

"Jesus commands us to pray for our enemies," said Ozgur, "Unless you change your attitude, I am walking away right now because you're letting Satan in the door. Pray for Gilley. You can't have resentment when you are praying for someone."

"No! Nothing would be more dishonest than me pretending that I want good to come to him. I want the wrath of God to fall on him!"

"You must!" said Ozgur, "It's Jesus' command! Think about it. If Gilley draws close to God, he'll be a changed person. He'll become more honest and more loving, he'll become a servant of God."

Daniel looked at Ozgur with anger and yet at the same time, he knew he was speaking the truth. He stared up to the clear blue sky again and said, "God, I pray that Gilley will wake up. He obviously doesn't know your love as he serves the god of money! He puts money above people! He can't know your love! Please reveal yourself to him and help me to forgive him!"

Daniel turned to Ozgur and said, "I'm trying."

Peace entered Daniel's mind. He paused and then said to Ozgur, "I want to dedicate this place to the Lord."

Ozgur nodded his head in agreement.

Daniel yelled out as loud as he could, "Have it God! Take this place. Let your will be done here!"

After a period of silence, Ozgur said, "So what should we call this place? Let's give it a name."

Daniel got up and said, "Have you heard of a 'City of Refuge'? God commanded the Hebrews to set up a City of Refuge. If a person was believed to be innocent when accused of murder, they could retreat to the city and be safe until the trial. Let's call this place, 'The City of Refuge.'"

Ozgur said, "The City of Refuge. I like it."

Daniel's thumb was feeling better. He turned to Ozgur and said, "I'm starting to like it here."

"Me too," said Ozgur.

"Let's get back to work."

ADDITIONAL PICTURES:

Cave Home, Moyen Bren, CC

The Underground City of Cappadocia

Cave Homes, LeticiaSouza, CC

Ancient church, Peter Simon, CC

Roman of Soldier and Slaves, Jun, CC

CHAPTER 2

CREATING COMMUNITY

Diocletian, CC

That evening, Daniel called a meeting to discuss the new project. Daniel and Ozgur were drafting some plans while Anasia prepared dinner. Suddenly there was a loud knock at the door. Anasia responded and was met by their friend Hermes. He had an obvious look of despair.

"What happened to you?" she asked.

After entering he said, "Some Roman officials showed up at the barracks and forced me to go to the temple, demanding that I worship that disgusting emperor. Of course, I refused. So, they fired me on the spot. They're firing all the Christians."

Hermes was an officer in the Roman military.

Daniel yelled from the next room, "Congratulations Hermes! You're a hero!"

Hermes walked over to Daniel and vented his anger, "I've got four children! What are we supposed to do? I don't have relatives that can take us in!"

Daniel said, "Yes you do! We're your family and we'll take you in!"

Hermes laughed and said, "How are you going to take on six people? You told us you must move out of here in a few days."

Daniel responded, "That's true, but God provides for his children."

Ozgur jumped into the conversation and said, "The same thing happened to me. They demanded I go worship Diocletian and I said, "Never!" They also fired me on the spot. Diocletian doesn't want any Christians working for the government."

Diocletian was the supreme emperor of the Roman Empire. He began requiring all government employees to worship him or face termination, knowing the Christians would refuse. He especially didn't want the Christians in the military, fearing that they would band together and form an uprising.

Daniel said to Hermes, "Today you were fired, but where is all this going? They're trying to strip us of our money and influence, but just wait."

Hermes replied, "I know. I heard that they enslaved one of the soldiers from my regiment. They said it was because he wasn't paying his taxes, but I don't believe it. He was a Christian."

Daniel responded, "How long are we going to sit and do nothing?"

Ozgur said, "And then there is Galerius. What happens when he takes over for Diocletian?"

Galerius was one of the four emperors that ruled over the Roman Empire. Diocletian shared some of his power with three other men, but as the supreme emperor, he ultimately called the shots. Galerius had recently married Diocletian's daughter, making him the prime candidate to succeed Diocletian. Rumors were circulating that Galerius had ruthlessly cut out the tongues of several Christians in his army. Many people believed that he could be the Antichrist.

Daniel said, "Hermes, Galerius is a real threat but here's the good news. I recently inherited a cave in the desert from my uncle. He endured the last round of persecution by hiding underground in this cave. It looks like a small cave, but it has several levels that go deep under the surface. Ozgur and I started chiseling and expanding. We are creating enough space so all of us can live and worship together down below. Huge stone doors will protect us from the Romans. The area surrounding the cave is perfect for cultivating and growing crops. We'll work the land at night. The women can make clothing that we will sell in town. If we ever fall under attack, we just seal up the entrance, and then we can survive for months. With our construction skills, we can do it!"

Anasia interjected, "We'll be an underground church!"

"That's right," said Daniel, "The underground church!"

Anasia said, "As we continue to seek the Lord and pray together, God will overcome the wicked Roman Empire. I am confident!"

Hermes said, "The Romans have been conquering and growing for 500 years! I wish I had your faith. I wish I believed that God is listening. If praying does anything, why is our world falling apart? Where is God right now? Look at you two. Look at all the Christians that have been devoured by the mouths of lions. Look at the Christians that have been turned into human torches! When is it going to end?"

Anasia said, "It will end when God says it is time for it to end. We need to trust in him and believe that he answers our prayers! Daniel and I started praying together and it has transformed our relationship. Then as soon as we decided to work on this project, more blessings started to flow into our lives. God has been filling us with a deeper sense of his peace and his presence! Given our circumstances, it makes no sense. Yet, God is giving us both victory!"

"You call this victory?" asked Hermes.

"Yes Hermes," said Anasia, "Believe it or not, our circumstances look horrible on the surface, but our problems have forced us to draw closer to God...and to one another. What could be better?"

Daniel smiled at his wife and then turned back to Hermes and said, "That's right Hermes. Don't ask why or how, but God is working among us."

Hermes could sense the passion and enthusiasm in the room.

"Hermes, come help with construction. You and your whole family can live there," said Daniel, "We're calling it, 'The City of Refuge'."

Ozgur interjected, "For the first time in a long time, I'm feeling hopeful. I went there today and was pleasantly surprised. The surrounding area is beautiful. Also, the cave has an underground well!"

"How many people are involved?" asked Hermes.

Daniel said, "Right now it is just us three," pointing to Ozgur, Anasia and himself.

"It sounds like a lot of work." said Hermes, "I have a better plan. Why don't we just start secretly killing Roman soldiers, picking them off one by one? I know how they operate from the inside."

Ozgur said, "Because God calls us to love our enemies. We all despise the Romans, but we live by a different set of rules. Besides, has any group been able to rebel against the Romans without being massacred?"

Daniel said, "The answer is an underground fortress! You know this, soldiers don't want to wait in the middle of nowhere for long. They will give up and move on if they ever discover us! The place is perfect. God's peace and his presence is there Hermes. He is with us!"

Anasia said, "What do you say Hermes? Come join us! We need you!"

After eating hot lentil soup, they prayed about the future and were all filled with a deeper sense of joy and peace. Hermes went home to his wife and explained everything to her. She was excited about packing up and moving. That very same night, Hermes informed Daniel that they wanted to commit to the effort.

The next morning, Daniel and Ozgur went to the market district to pick up some new tools. As they approached the tool merchant's stand, Daniel noticed Cyprian, the local tax collector. He was standing in his black toga alongside two Roman soldiers. Daniel tried to avoid eye contact as they slipped by.

The tool merchant was a Christian. Daniel grabbed the tools that he needed and placed them in front of the shop owner. The man asked quietly, "What are you working on Daniel?"

"I need you to keep it a secret," said Daniel in a very low tone.

The shop owner nodded his head in agreement.

"We're building an underground haven with a group of believers. A relative has some extra property."

"An underground haven? Why?" asked the shop owner.

"Why?" Daniel whispered, "Is your head in the sand?"

"Daniel," said the shop owner, "There are too many Christians now. What are they going to do? Start killing us all? The Romans are kicking some of the Christians out of the military. Big deal. It makes sense because most Christians won't fight anyway. You're acting on your fears."

"No," said Daniel firmly, "It started with the military. Now they are firing us from all government jobs. Ozgur was just fired. You know he is an architect and a hard worker. They are doing everything they can to strip us of our power...little by little."

"Daniel, don't read too much into it," said the shop owner with a blank look on his face. He then said, "That will be four denarii."

Daniel replied, "Just a few days ago you said it was two denarii."

"Daniel, everything is going up," responded the shop owner. Inflation is rampant throughout the empire. If I charge any less, I'll lose money."

Daniel handed him the coins and said, "If you ever need help, look for us."

After the two men started walking away, the tax collector yelled, "Daniel! Get over here now!"

The men walked over to Cyprian. He was very tall and overweight with a round stern face, bald head, and a short graying beard.

Cyprian asked, "What are you working on Daniel? It's obvious that you have a project! Look at me in the eyes! Do you have a project?"

"A relative's home," said Daniel, while trying to calm himself. "No commercial projects for me right now. No money changing hands, this I can assure you."

Cyprian responded, "Oh yeah? You Christians are such liars! Remember, we're keeping a watchful eye on both of you. It's not just money Daniel, you can't barter labor for goods. We know that game. We're not foolish!"

"I promise. We are not working on any paid jobs. We would gladly take care of our taxes if that were the case," said Daniel.

"Then how are you surviving? Where are you getting your money Daniel? You still owe me back taxes. And where did you get the money for those tools?"

"From my relatives," said Daniel. "My wife's family is supporting us right now and we are fixing my uncle's cave. Cyprian, you know I've lost everything, my house is gone and I'm out of the project for the Inn with Gilley. He has my house, and we are destitute."

Cyprian then turned to Ozgur and moved close to his face, "Are you also working on his uncle's cave?" he asked.

Ozgur said, "Yes sir."

"For free?" asked Cyprian, "Don't play me as a fool! Nobody works for free!"

"I'm helping a good friend," said Ozgur calmly. "I just lost my job and what else am I going to do?"

"No compensation!" screamed Cyprian as people in the surrounding area looked on, "If I hear of either of you doing anything for money without paying taxes, I will not hesitate to throw shackles on both of you! Do you hear me! I'm sure you'll enjoy working in the mines!"

Terror seized them both, thinking about Bildau and knowing that Cyprian had followed through on his threats.

"You can't get paid for anything! Not even with a loaf of bread! Do you hear me! No working without paying taxes!"

Daniel said, "Yes sir. We are following the law and will continue to do so."

The two walked away. Daniel looked at Ozgur and said, "We're moving into the City of Refuge first thing tomorrow morning."

"I'll join you," said Ozgur.

They walked a short distance to the home of Nicolas, Daniel's mentor, and a leader in his church.

Daniel's church had recently fallen apart when Justin, the lead Pastor, divorced his good Christian wife after it was discovered that he was having multiple affairs. He planned to continue his job as the pastor and marry another woman. Many of the believers feared that his behavior would spread and become an acceptable practice. Nicolas had confronted Justin, but the man was unrepentant. He then broke away from all the other churches to form his own sect.

After the incident, Nicolas reached out to Daniel because he saw that he had discipline and great leadership skills, He hoped that one day Daniel could replace Justin if he could just get his marriage on track.

The two knocked on Nicolas' door and were greeted by a smiling weathered face. Daniel said, "I hope you don't mind that I brought Ozgur."

"Certainly not," said Nicolas, as the three men shook hands. Nicolas invited them in and then brought out some hot fresh bread and a sweet mint drink. Daniel shared his plans to move to The City of Refuge.

Nicolas responded as he poured the drink, "Daniel, I'm hearing chilling reports about Galerius. It's time to act. I've had two meetings with Roman officials recently and I'm worried. They keep arriving and asking random questions. There's something going on. I'll probably be joining you."

"Yes!" exclaimed Daniel, "We need your wisdom and quite frankly, we need money and supplies. Do you know anyone willing to contribute?"

"I know some believers that might want to help," said Nicolas, "I'll get back to you on this."

"You are well aware of my situation," said Daniel, "I can't work. Any money that I make goes toward my fake tax bill. It's time for me to go into seclusion, but we need money to survive."

Afterwards, Nicolas decided to visit the City of Refuge. Upon seeing the interior, he decided to join Daniel and Ozgur. The three men became the decision-making team for The City of Refuge.

In just a few weeks they had over 80 people living together down below. Nicolas secured finances and they began to stockpile supplies.

It took some time, but they completed the worship area and held a special ceremony, pouring anointing oil over the entrance to the room. One of the men was a talented artist and he began to create murals on the walls of the room, depicting scenes from the scriptures.

Nicolas addressed the group on that first meeting, pointing to a newly created mural. He said, "I was reading about the three young Jews, Shadrach, Meshach, and Abednego from the scriptures. Now we have a picture on the wall describing the story."

Nicolas pointed to the image that displayed three men, ornately dressed in purple, standing in fire.

He said, "When the Jews were living in Babylon about 600 years before the birth of Christ, estranged from their native land of Israel, the king's advisors created a law that forced everyone to worship a statue of the Babylonian King. The three young Jewish men refused and were thrown into the fiery furnace! The king was there to watch. He looked in and saw not just three men in the fire, but four! He said there was one like the 'son of man' in the furnace along with the three. God performed a miracle, and the three young men survived the fierce heat!

"When Jesus walked the earth, he called himself the 'son of man.' He was the Son of God, but he also called himself the son of man. I believe that this person in the furnace with the three was no other than Jesus himself! God has given us an example from the past for us today. God is with us in the fire, and he will get us through this fire of persecution! May he be with us down here!

"Diocletian and Galerius are mere men! They seek power and are willing to harm and kill anyone that stands in their way! They want us to worship them! Will we? Will we ever worship them? The answer is clearly and unequivocally no! Never! We might have to enter the furnace, but the Lord will be with us in the fire!

"Did you know that the angels are empowered as we fast and pray? They can defeat the enemies that stand against us! The book of Revelation describes our prayers as incense before the Lord! As we pray earnestly, humbling ourselves before God, He will fight for us and break through the darkness! The angels will defeat the devil and the principalities that stand over the Roman Empire! Circumstances look bad, but our God is so much greater than our circumstances! In an instant, everything can change as we repent and pray!"

Everyone applauded and they were all greatly encouraged. After a sincere time of prayer, they ate together in the newly created dining area, feasting on slow cooked lamb and vegetables with fresh hot bread.

Hermes was sitting next to Daniel and said, "I was feeling defeated, but now I sense that God is truly at work. I can taste victory on some level. Daniel, thank you for all that you and your wife are doing."

Daniel replied, "You are welcome my brother. All glory to God. This is his work!"

That evening, Daniel went to bed in his little apartment. Anasia looked at him as they cuddled and said, "I really believe that God has led us here. I feel safe. When we were living in town, I constantly feared that someone would come at any time and take you away." She then said, "but that could have been a good thing actually now that I think about it!"

"Hey!" said Daniel, as the two laughed.

"It's amazing here," said Anasia. I'm so proud of you."

Daniel replied, "As strange as it may sound, I'm happier than I've ever been."

Anasia said to him, "Do you want to pray?"

The two prayed together, thanking God for their new home and their friends. Then Anasia blew out the lamp and they began to kiss passionately.

Anasia was haunted by her barren womb and felt like she was cursed. In the past, she would get jealous of other women with families and children, showing obvious anger in their presence. In The City of Refuge, she started helping the women with children. On a regular basis, she would teach kids how to read and write. She experienced incredible joy as she began to serve the other families, and she was filled with hope that the next generation would be educated and spread the gospel.

With Ozgur's engineering skills, they built huge round stone doors to protect themselves from attack. The doors had a hole in the middle so they could shoot arrows through the narrow corridor if they were invaded. They placed one of these doors on each level. If anyone was able to penetrate one door, they had many others that they would have to break through.

They also chiseled out several vents, allowing for the flow of fresh air from above. Ozgur got a brilliant idea and turned one of the vents into a secret lookout. Residents could crawl up and down the vent using slots in the wall for climbing. They could view the entrance by looking through a small hole in one of the rocks on the surface.

One day, as they were excavating a new room, Ozgur discovered yellow smelly crystals in the rock. He ran to tell Daniel and asked, "Is this what I think it is?"

Daniel took a sniff and exclaimed, "Oh my! I believe it is sulfur!"

After they lit the rock on fire and smelled the horrific odor, "Daniel exclaimed, "Oh yah, it's sulfur alright!"

Ozgur showed Daniel the area where he made the discovery. After perusing the abundant crystals in the rock, Daniel exclaimed, "Oh my! God has given us an endless supply of sulfur!"

Additional Pictures:

Four Emperors, Nino Barbieri, CC

Shadrach, Meshach and Abednego
Early Church Painting, CC

Air vent with slots for climbing, Nevit, CC

CHAPTER 3

GALERIUS

Galerius, Canellolous CC

February 22, 303AD

In one year after Daniel and Ozgur began their work on The City of Refuge, their number grew to over 100 residents. Life in The City of Refuge had its challenges, but everybody made the most of it.

One day Anasia returned from the market area in Cappadocia after selling some clothing. Daniel was standing by the entrance of the city when she hysterically ran up.

She exclaimed, "I just saw Galerius! We were in town, and we wanted to cross the street, but we were forced to wait as a massive army marched by. Suddenly, the officials announced that the emperor was passing and demanded that we all bow down. I didn't want to do it! The man said he would arrest me if I didn't bow down!"

Daniel held her in his arms.

"I did it! Does this mean I've worshipped him?" She fearfully asked.

"No! No!" said Daniel, "Of course not! All are required to bow down before a Roman Emperor, but that's not the same as worshiping him."

"Good," she said, as she began to smile.

"It's okay," assured Daniel, "To worship him is to proclaim that he is a god."

Galerius had been engaged in a war with the king of Persia to the east. After winning the conflict, he traveled through Cappadocia on his way to celebrate his triumph in Nicaea with a victory parade.

Nicaea was several hundred miles northwest of Cappadocia. Diocletian had proclaimed this city the new center of power for the entire Roman Empire, moving it away from Rome in Italy for the first time in 500 years.

The King of Persia had invaded a region just east of Cappadocia. A year before this event, Galerius had fought the same king and suffered a humiliating defeat. Then the King of Persia advanced to take more land and a new war erupted. If Galerius lost a second time, he would have been denied the top tier position as the supreme emperor of the Roman Empire. With the help of a brilliant young warrior named Constantine, the dreaded emperor stood victorious, cementing his ascension as the most powerful man in the world.

The following week Galerius stood at the gate of Nicaea in his chariot, waiting for his parade to begin. The pinnacle experience for a Roman Emperor was his victory procession. The governors and officials of the vast Roman Empire were called in to celebrate his win. Galerius could hear commotion coming from inside the city. His heart throbbed with excitement.

He reflected on his previous defeat against the Persians from the year before. Diocletian forced Galerius to walk through the streets, publicly ridiculing him with every degrading name mentionable. Now this time, he had won the war and was eager to take revenge on his father-in-law.

Some soldiers were fixing a wheel on one of the carriages, holding up start of the parade. Galerius was becoming increasingly impatient.

He finally screamed, "Fix it right now or there will be hell to pay!" He jumped down from his chariot and began to hit the men with his horse whip. He then kicked one of the soldiers in the shoulder and exclaimed "Forget about using this carriage! Let's go!"

Galerius got back on his chariot and yelled, "It's time to begin!"

One of his commanders nodded his head in agreement as he signaled for the procession to commence.

The gate suddenly opened as the emperor fought for control of his four gigantic white horses. Galerius barely managed to maintain composure, but it looked spectacular with the horses lunging forward. The crowd erupted with a deafening roar, as the people lining the street suddenly bowed down before Galerius, looking up to catch a glimpse as he passed by.

Galerius was brutally handsome, while standing a foot taller than all the other men in his parade. He had dark vacant eyes and black hair with a thick muscular body. His blazing purple toga eclipsed all the other fanfare of the parade. The dye that created the special toga was the most expensive substance known to man, more valuable than jewels or gold, worn exclusively by the emperors of Rome.

Just behind Galerius, was Constantine, much shorter than Galerius, but equally good looking with a hooked nose and a distinctive split chin. He had a perpetual cheerful smile and bright blue eyes that he inherited from his mother Helena.

Constantine was being mentored by Diocletian while living in his palace. He had been weaned from his youth to become an emperor. Now that he had just turned 20, Diocletian asked Galerius to give Constantine opportunity to prove himself on the battlefield, which he did.

He stood as the only real challenge to Galerius (5). Galerius pretended to assist him, when in fact, he was hopeful that Constantine would die. He had given him an impossible task, and yet Constantine succeeded. All the men favored Constantine and were empowered by his mere presence. He had natural fighting skills and was a brilliant strategist.

Behind Constantine was a caged carriage carrying seven scantily dressed Persian women. These were the concubines and the wife of the King of Persia. Many of the men of the crowd stormed forward, fighting for a closer look. Behind the women, 2,000 members of Galerius' army marched in perfect formation.

It was rumored the Romans would publicly display one of their catapults for the very first time. To the delight of the crowd, it was true! The large mechanism made loud squeaking noises as it was towed by two large horses. The catapults had given the Romans a significant advantage in battle, surprising their opponents with fuel filled bombs that released flames of horror and death.

They stopped the procession. One of the soldiers carried the torch and lit one of the bombs seated on the catapult. They released the mechanism wherein the catapult arm hurled the fireball hundreds of feet. It landed in an empty field, causing a huge explosion. The crowd was shocked. The power was inconceivable.

At the end of the procession, bloody whips cracked as ten captured Persian soldiers were herded along. Children from the crowd were hurling rocks at the shackled prisoners. These men were the choicest Persian warriors and had earned the opportunity to extend their lives by a few months as gladiators in the coliseum.

Galerius stopped in front of Diocletian's palace and slowly exited his chariot. He then spoke to Constantine, "Don't take a step until I make it to the top of the staircase."

Diocletian stood at the top of the steps along with his daughter, Galerius' wife. Diocletian was once a mighty warrior, but at 58 years old, he was barely able to stand in his diseased state. His right hand was shaking, and his stomach was constantly erupting with pain. It was becoming embarrassing for him to be seen in public. He was worshipped as a god and yet, here he was on display as a feeble man. The illusion of immortality that had given him so much power was quickly fading away.

All the men that surrounded Diocletian fantasized about standing in his position. Oh, to have his palace, his food and especially his concubines. He could get whatever he wanted, whenever he wanted it. Diocletian's instincts told him that he was constantly in danger of a coup. Many of Rome's most powerful emperors died at the hands of power-seeking men. The stress of managing the Roman Empire and living in the fear of an assassination had taken its toll.

Diocletian whispered to himself as he watched Galerius ascend the steps, "Get ready for battle."

Before he had given his daughter away in marriage, Galerius had been respectful and charming, but immediately after the wedding ceremony, he was given license to display his true self.

Halfway up the stairs, Galerius stopped when he saw the newly erected church just above the palace. He stared at it for several seconds and then shook his head with an obvious look of disgust.

When he made his way to the top, Diocletian reached out his hand, making an honorable gesture to his son-in-law. Galerius grasped it for a second, but then quickly let go. He then proceeded to kiss his wife, having completed her duty, she walked away. They hadn't seen each other for over a year, but it didn't matter to either of them. It was a gesture for the crowd.

Diocletian said, "Congratulations Galerius," He pointed to the seven women in the cage and said in jest, "And thank you for your gracious gift!"

Galerius said, "They're my slaves Diocletian. Only a fool would waste such beauty on a weak old man."

Diocletian was greatly angered and said slowly, "What should we do with you Galerius?"

"They are the spoils of victory!" boasted Galerius, "Yes, victory this time!"

Diocletian said, "I heard that you have little to show for your so-called victory. Only your new concubines and a few gladiators. No gold, no slaves. You are going to bankrupt the empire! You don't deserve the victory march!"

Galerius knew that he had failed to support the empire, but he deflected Diocletian's counterattacks by pointing to the church and saying, "I heard that you allowed the Christians to build their temple right above your palace. I could not believe it was true! Now I have seen it with my own eyes. Surely you have upset the gods and they have cursed your body!"

Diocletian looked up into the air and said, "The battle begins," as he shook his head and then looked at his advisors. Both he and Galerius knew that he didn't have much fight left in him.

The church leaders took a risk by constructing their building so close to the palace. They were hoping that it might impact Diocletian. At times he would listen to the singing from his balcony, and it did intrigue him. His wife and daughter had begun to secretly meet with some of the Christians.

One of Diocletian's servants walked up and bowed before the supreme emperor. He said, "Your eminence, the meal is ready."

Galerius along with three of his top men walked into the dining area.

They all sat down at the large table. Diocletian had three of his trusted advisors sit with him along with Constantine and a Roman priest, opposite Galerius and several governors.

The guards looked on and imagined themselves gorging on the luscious cheeses, braised meats and other delicacies displayed before their eyes. The trusted cupbearer tasted the food as Diocletian stared at him with intensity.

One of Diocletian's cupbearers had died the week before.

After a few minutes, an advisor shook his head and the men started eating, but Diocletian had lost his appetite and could feel anxiety rising.

One of the local governors said to Galerius, "We've heard different reports, give us the details of your triumph."

Galerius began by saying, "When we located the Persian King, I ordered my best men to infiltrate his camp at night. Miraculously, they captured the King's entire harem and his wife! The ultimate treasure trove! You saw the women in the parade! Perfection!" (1)

Diocletian interrupted, "I heard that Constantine had proven himself once again and that he and his men had infiltrated the camp?"

"Yes, but he was just doing as I commanded him!" exclaimed Galerius looking at Constantine. "He and his men performed brilliantly as they carried out my plans."

In fact, the entire plot was all Constantine's idea. Constantine fought with himself not to say anything.

Galerius then continued, "The next day I sent messengers to the Persian king, informing him that the women would be amid our archers and catapults during battle. I told him the precise time of our attack. I figured the fool would be selfish, willing to sacrifice his men to preserve his women. And you know what? I was right! He ordered his men not to shoot arrows or catapults at us, giving us a huge advantage! They had no idea of our capabilities with our equipment! Nothing is more delightful than to watch your enemies scramble around in flames at the start of a battle with no recourse! We completely obliterated his forces and the king fled to the Tigris!

"It was payback time for last year," continued Galerius, "You remember last year Diocletian? Oh yah, you remember it well. Remember dragging me through the streets of Nicaea and calling me every humiliating name your sick mind could conjure up."

Diocletian continued to eat with his head down. Galerius then signaled one of his men to hand him the treaty from the King of Persia. He held it up before everyone.

"After they surrendered, the foolish Persian King demanded his wife and concubines be returned!" said Galerius while laughing. "He was in no position to negotiate. Besides, I deserved some trophies for my victory. After the king fled the scene and the rest of them surrendered, I realized that there were just too many Persian prisoners. I lined the enemy up in rows and tied their hands and feet behind. Then I ordered that they all be killed."

Diocletian said, "That was a mistake! You should have saved them and brought them back! The empire desperately needs slaves!"

Galerius completely ignored his father-in-law and continued, "I heard that one of my captains refused to follow orders. He was brought into my presence as he explained that he had become a Christian. He said that he needed to 'love his enemies.' He said, 'They surrendered in good faith, and we must be men of honor.'

Galerius said, 'I thought, 'No, not again. This disease is spreading everywhere!' I grabbed my sword and had two men hold him while I personally chopped off his head."

Diocletian said, "You realize Galerius, that this war and its expenses will bankrupt the empire!"

Galerius again deflected Diocletian's attack. He turned to speak only to Diocletian, "I'm asking myself why are we even fighting? The enemy stands right here destroying the empire from within! The Persians won't be bothering us for a long time, but we are still at war!"

Diocletian tried to say something, but the pain in his stomach prevented him from responding.

Galerius began his charged assault on Diocletian, "I just can't believe that you would allow them to build one of their Christian temples right above your palace! You're not only physically sick Diocletian, but you've also lost your mind! Do you know that in their meetings they pray for a new kingdom to come! They make their own laws, challenging our government! They bring only shame and guilt to their followers and everyone else! It's a sick and disgusting belief system that is ruining the empire! And now they put one of their buildings above your palace! What does that say to the masses?"

"What do you want Galerius!" yelled Diocletian. The Supreme Roman Emperor felt waves of heaviness rolling over him as his anger burned.

"I want you to do something!" countered Galerius, "How can the empire continue while these rebels take over? All our problems are ultimately because of them! If we don't respond hard and fast right now, they will dominate us! I fear that the empire will be finished forever!"

Diocletian said, "We've taken action against them."

"You have thrown a teaspoon of water on a blazing fire! You might be firing them from a few government posts, but the converts are everywhere!" countered Galerius. "And besides, if you force them from government jobs and they're not working, then they will spend more of their time converting the masses! Everything you have done has just made the problem worse!"

Diocletian paused.

Constantine's mother Helena moved closer to the dining room to listen to the discussion.

Diocletian then yelled at the top of his lungs, "What do you want from me Galerius?!"

"A solution Diocletian!" countered Galerius, "I demand a solution!"

"And what are you proposing as a solution?" asked Diocletian.

Galerius did not respond.

"What is your solution?" Diocletian demanded.

"Extermination," said Galerius.

An incredulous look of shock appeared on the faces of everyone in the room.

Diocletian shook his head in disgust and stood up, "Are you mad?"

Galerius arose from the table and started walking around, looking at all the other officials, "Anyone unwilling to bow down before the emperor of Rome is an enemy of the Roman Empire. This has been the law for hundreds of years! We have gone soft!"

"You can't just start killing all the Christians!" said Diocletian.

"Yes, I can, and I will!" said Galerius, as he paused as if trying to contain his anger. He pointed his finger at Diocletian and continued, "When I have an enemy, I kill him! That is what a man does! A worm does nothing!"

All the officials stared at Diocletian, waiting for his response as he looked for a way out.

He responded awkwardly by saying, "Let's send someone to the Oracle of Apollo and see what he says about the Christians." He turned to the priest standing by the table and said, "Go and meet the Oracle. Ask him what we should do about the Christians."

Galerius and Diocletian said nothing while they ate and waited for the priest to return. A short while later he appeared back and said, "The Oracle has spoken."

"And what does he say?" asked Galerius.

He says, 'The righteous ones of the earth are preventing him from speaking the truth.'"

"What is that supposed to mean?" demanded Diocletian.

One of Diocletian's advisors asked, "Who are the righteous ones?"

The priest answered, "The Christians of course."

Galerius rushed in and said, "You see! The Christians! Their power is growing and now the Oracle can't even hear the gods because of them!" (2)

Diocletian said, "I want to know why they are called 'The righteous?'"

Galerius ignored Diocletian's question and screamed, "Why do you keep defending them? Are you now a Christian? Are you one of them? That must be it!"

Diocletian responded, "Of course not!" as the officials stared at him. "But I want to know why they are called the righteous."

"Why would you defend them?" asked Galerius. "If you have become a Christian then you must hand over your power to me right now. The Roman Empire cannot be controlled by a Christian!"

"I am not defending them and of course I have not converted," declared Diocletian.

"You have converted," said Galerius, "Otherwise you would take action!"

"Alright! I've had it!" yelled Diocletian, "Kill the Christians! Kill all of them!"

Diocletian sat down and stared at his food. His intestines were causing him horrendous pain, as if someone was jabbing him with a knife.

Galerius said to Diocletian, "Do you want me to prepare the edict, or will you do it for us?"

Diocletian said, "Prepare the document and I will sign it," struggling to say the words.

Diocletian realized that despite all his victories, he was depleted and empty. He had forced his way to the top of the world. He thought he had everything, but his pursuits had cheated him of peace of mind and health. He looked around at the people in the room, each manipulating for power. He was hit with the realization that he would soon die if he continued to play this game.

The first goal of a Roman emperor was to provide for the needs of the military and acquire slaves. When the Romans conquered a new area, they would enslave the women along with the defeated soldiers while stealing the treasures of the land. Expansion fed the empire. Without expansion, the empire would die.

By waging war against the Christians, the empire could conquer from within. By making the Christians appear as the enemy of Rome, they could confiscate the property of the Christians, gain revenue, and have fresh slave labor which included female sexual slaves for the soldiers.

From the very beginning of the Roman Empire, expansion was essential. In 750 BC, Rome was nothing more than a swampy village with a population of 3000 people. Romulus, the leader of this village, decided to allow anyone trying to escape slavery or debt to move to his village. It became a 'City of Refuge.'

His village grew quickly, and the residents respected Romulus for his help. But only men were coming to his city which created a shortage of women. Romulus therefore developed a solution.

He invited the Sabines, the people from a neighboring region over to his city for a festival. In the middle of the event, they captured the young Sabine women, about 400 of them. After the abduction, they forced the men to leave. Several months later, the Sabines formed an army and came back to fight Romulus' village and retake their women. The captured Sabine women supposedly threw themselves into the center of the battle, stopping the fight. They then cried out to their former husbands, pleading with them to allow them to stay with their new men.

Romulus turned to the Sabine King and promised that they could replace the women, if they would just unite and take over the surrounding areas. The two groups chose to expand as one, forgetting the transgression while creating a partnership. After Romulus died, the Sabine King took over the leadership position and the empire continued to expand quickly.

The Romans would surprise their enemies with their inconceivable acts of cruelty, creating fear before and during battle. They would defeat kings, crucify, or enslave the enemy soldiers and then set up puppet governments. The people willing to work with the Romans would become government officials and tax collectors. Many times, these people would conspire with the Romans before they took over a region, sabotaging the government from within, but ensured a position of power once victory was complete. (3)

It was almost impossible for a region to break away from the grip of Rome once they were conquered. If there was any hint or accusation of rebellion, immediate torture, slavery, or death awaited the accused.

Galerius said, "We will release an edict called, 'The Edict Against the Christians' and we will celebrate the new era with a feast. We'll call it 'The Feast of the Termination.' The Christians have a festival when they believe their leader came back to life. We will hold our feast on that very same day and begin the greatest purge in history!" (4)

The Roman priest interjected, "We need to do everything possible to obtain their writings! People convert when they read their books. It is as if their books have some magical influence. If we destroy their books, we strip them of their power forever!"

"Fine," said Diocletian, "Do whatever you want. I don't care anymore." He looked around at all the men surrounding him and yelled, "Do you hear me? I don't care!"

Galerius stood up and said, "I do care." He then looked at the men in the room and said, "And I'm glad that there are others that still care."

As Galerius exited, he stopped to stare at Constantine. After giving the young man a look of disdain and hatred, he left the palace.

Constantine saw his mother Helena and then spoke privately to her. At one time Helena was the favorite sexual slave of Constanine's father, Constantius, the emperor for the region above Italy. Normally, a slave would be forced to have an abortion when pregnant. However, Helena was able to persuade her master to permit her to give birth and then be given freedom. She kept a watchful eye on the boy and reported his progress to his father while he was being weaned to become an emperor.

Constantine asked, "Why do people hate the Christians so? I don't understand."

Helena asked Constantine, "Have you ever talked to a Christian?"

Constantine replied, "No, but I heard they drink blood and eat human flesh in their ceremonies."

Helena responded, "That is a lie Constantine. The Christians only want to bring love into the world. Those given over to hate will always come against the source of love. Jesus, the one they call the Christ did nothing but help and love people. He miraculously healed the sick and explained the true ways of God. They perform a ritual using bread and wine, but they never eat human flesh."

"Wait a second," said Constantine, "Why are you defending them?"

She said, "Constantine, my view of the world has changed. Just two weeks ago, I was talking to one of my maids. I was wondering why the Christians were willing to suffer for their beliefs. She told me the stories about Jesus, and something erupted in my soul. I can't put it into words Constantine. Jesus took all the sin of the world upon himself when he was killed. Jesus was crucified at the hands of the Jews and the Roman Empire but was resurrected! Now, he is living inside of me and all the Christians! He is the lamb that was sacrificed for us! This Jewish man from Israel is the true Son of God! I have found what I've been looking for all my life!"

Constantine was shaking his head in disbelief as he whispered, "Mother be quiet. You've gone mad."

"Constantine, your mother is now a Christian," she said quietly with a confident boldness, "I am not making any apologies. I know that the timing couldn't be worse, but how can I escape the truth? Should I be afraid of these men over the Creator?"

Constantine said, "Don't you know what you are up against?"

"Yes," she said with a smile, "but in light of God's love, I am willing to go to any length, even death."

"That is ridiculous. What did they do to you?" asked Constantine.

"Nothing," she said, "My maid talked to me. I realized she was speaking the truth. I went to someone's house, and they baptized me in their bath, which means they simply dunked me in the water."

"Was this some type of special water?" asked Constantine.

"No," she said, "It was just normal water."

Constantine asked, "How could it be just normal water. Did you read their writings? I've heard not to ever read their writings! Ever! There is a magic spell that comes on those who read their books."

"Yes," said Helena, "They're just stories that include the teachings of Jesus the Christ. You must read them."

"No!" said Constantine, "Never!" Smiling as a servant walked by to not draw attention to their conversation. He stared at his mother with anger for several seconds. A look of confusion then came over him as he walked away.

In the city of Philadelphia, a hundred miles to the west of Cappadocia, two young couples were walking home from church on a Sunday. At their morning service, the minister had announced that he had received word of coming persecution. The two couples were desperately creating a plan of action.

Antoney had recently married his wife, Calista. He was a successful spice trader, having inherited his family's business.

The other couple, Val, and his wife Sasa had a young girl and worked together selling fabric.

Val said to the others, "All of us must move to Cappadocia at once. The believers there all work together to protect themselves."

Sasa said, "We know people there."

They passed by two Roman soldiers that were standing guard along the road. The soldiers had been waiting for Calista, knowing that she would be walking home from church right at that moment.

"There she is!" said one of the soldiers. Then they proceeded to follow the two couples.

"Oh my! Hey beautiful," yelled the other soldier.

"She is one in ten million," said his friend, laughing like a preying hyena.

Calista was perhaps the most attractive woman in the entire region. With her prominent features and perfect curves, she caused an eruption of emotion in every man that glanced at her. When she was a child, her family had to hide her from the public officials, fearing that they would take her away for temple service. The beautiful virgin women of the land were forced to live in the Roman temples until 30 years of age. Her parents insisted that she marry young so she would be released from the threat of service.

Beauty was a blessing and a curse. She always kept her head covered and wore unattractive fabric, looking down as she walked to avoid conflict.

There was word among the soldiers that they would have free reign to plunder the Christians. They would have freedom to rob, rape and enslave, and so they were preparing their move.

Sasa said quietly, "They have no dignity."

Val whispered, "But they have swords. Don't say anything Sasa, just keep walking."

Calista said quietly to Antoney, "Please, let's leave Philadelphia right away."

"Yes," said Antoney, "I'm getting everything together. We will leave shortly."

Anxiety was high for all of them.

ADDITIONAL PICTURES:

Nicaea City Gate, Quarterlatin CC

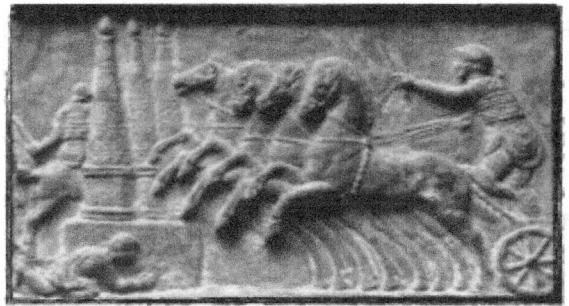
Roman Emperor's Chariot, CC

Constantine, Camile King, CC

CHAPTER 4

THE WAR

Roman Bull Sacrifice, Wolfgang Sauber, CC

A few weeks later, all four emperors were brought together in Nicaea to celebrate the 'Feast of the Termination.' Adorned in their brilliant purple togas, they stood in a circle in the temple courtyard. The four men argued with each other about increasing taxes and the other challenges facing the empire.

Their wives stood together in another circle a few feet away. Most of the men had concubines and their wives existed merely for public appearances. After fathering a child through their wives, the emperors always preferred their collection of beautiful young concubines.

The main priest entered the courtyard area in his white robe and announced, "We are beginning the ceremony. Enter the temple at once!"

The emperors were escorted to the front row of the building as they sat down with their wives. After a few minutes, the mystic horns and harps began to play as flawless temple virgins entered and danced in perfect harmony. The Romans understood the power of beauty to win the hearts of the masses. When men entered the Roman temples, they experienced the intoxicating appearance of these women. Women as well were intrigued by the appearance of these select 'virgins.' The vestal virgins, as they were called, loved their lives of ease and comfort, consumed only with maximizing their appearance.

Outside the temple, lifelike statues of the virgins lined the entrance, luring the men inside whenever they walked by.

The Roman priest walked up to the front and began his discourse on the evils of Christianity. He proclaimed that the gods that had made Rome great were outraged, angered that the Christians were allowed to flourish. He said that the economy was suffering because of what he called, the 'Christian Curse.' He announced that Galerius' recent victory over the Persians was a direct result of the purges of the Christians from the government, but that more needed to be done. He ended by announcing his complete support for the decision to attack the Christians.

Christianity was clearly jeopardizing the priest's power. The thought of losing his place of influence to the Christians was unbearable. His life of ease and pleasure was in jeopardy. His favorite responsibility was to protect the vestal virgins. Under his watch, he made sure that none of the temple virgins were true virgins, silencing them with the threat of death if they ever spoke up. Another one of his jobs was to scout for young virgins to join him in the temple, knowing that in time they would be his for the taking.

His greatest fear was that if the Christians continued to grow in influence, they would shut down the system that fed his sexual appetites.

At the end of the ceremony, the head priest took a lamb as all the emperors stood together. Diocletian placed his hand on the lamb, making a passionless gesture as the priest pierced the animal with his knife. Only the supreme leader could receive a lamb sacrifice. This was the act that set him apart from the others, making him a 'god.'

Galerius looked on with unbridled enthusiasm, enamored by the realization that very soon he would receive a lamb sacrifice and be worshipped as a god. In just a short while, all mankind would bow down before him or face death.

For as long as he had been in the military, he fantasized about that moment. The people from his childhood that made fun of him, that hurt him, that turned on him, would soon suffer wrath. He believed that when he became the supreme emperor, he could have anything or anyone, for pleasure, or revenge, thus alleviating his soul from the torments he experienced.

Galerius was born the illegitimate son of a prostitute, a woman of low reputation, the brunt of many jokes and the topic of much conversation in his town. Those that stared at him when he would walk by as a child would now die. All those people from his past that caused him any bit of pain would experience torture and death. He fantasized about traveling back to his hometown for this very reason.

The priest called everybody up to the altar to offer prayers to the gods of Rome. Priscilla, the wife of Diocletian, had a conversation with Helena about Jesus a couple of days before the feast. She believed in her core that Helena's words were true, but she was too afraid to act, knowing that it would probably cost her everything.

Now here she was, at a ceremony to celebrate the termination of the Christians. As Priscilla walked to the front of the temple, she could feel the evil surrounding her, penetrating her goodness. She looked in front of her and stared at Galerius as he walked up to the altar. He was attractive and strong, the kind of person that would make a Mother-In-Law proud, but at this moment, she could

The War

feel his wickedness. In fact, everything around her seemed pathetically evil, suffocating any love within her. She knew that she was part of a diabolical force.

Priscilla longed to run away but continued forward because of her desire to maintain the approval of all those around her (6). She prostrated herself and offered prayers to the gods of Rome. Immediately afterward, she ran outside, away from all the people. Disgusted and crying, she vowed to separate herself completely from the ways of the empire. Priscilla chose at this moment to talk further with Helena and become a Christian, no matter the cost.

After the ceremony, the emperors and statesmen were all enjoying the food and drink for the 'Feast of the Termination'. Galerius was sitting next to Diocletian. He looked at him and said, "You need to retire Diocletian. It's obvious that the demands of the empire are killing you. When should we expect you to call it quits?"

Diocletian said, "Three years, hopefully less."

Galerius responded, "I don't see how you can last three years. Really? You must let it all go."

Following the ceremony, the four emperors took a carriage to Diocletian's palace. The first order of business was to destroy the church just above the imperial palace. In the middle of their Resurrection Sunday service, everyone exited the building to watch 5000 Roman soldiers preparing for their *attack*. (6.5)

"What is happening?" said one of the Christians, while watching the men assemble.

"It's true, the rumors are true!" said Marcellus, the overseer of the church.

"Tell everyone to flee now!" yelled one of the deacons.

"Yes, but I'm going to remain right here," said Marcellus.

The deacon yelled, "No Marcellus, it's just a building! You are not helping anyone if you let them kill you!"

Marcellus wouldn't listen. He had worked hard to construct the building and had made it into something of an idol. He was a Roman priest that had converted, forsaking the Roman god's and temples. However, he transferred his Roman beliefs over to his Christian beliefs and just like the Romans, he put too much emphasis on the beauty of the building.

The deacon quoted the Apostle Paul to Marcellus, he said, "Paul stood in Athens before the temple there and said, "The God who made the world and everything in it is the Lord of heaven and earth and does not live in temples built by human hands!" Come Marcellus. It's just a building!"

"No! It's not just a building!" said Marcellus, "It is the house of God!"

Down the hill, Galerius and the emperors stood on the balcony of Diocletian's palace. Galerius said to Diocletian, "I must address the troops."

Diocletian agreed but he said, "Just make sure they don't use fire! You must protect the surrounding buildings!"

Galerius shook his head. He then went in front of the men and yelled, "Quiet!"

He waited for silence and then began his speech. The soldiers stood in complete attention.

"For too long the disease called Christianity has been infecting the Roman Empire. Weak leadership within our ranks allowed these

The War

rats to fester. The enemy appears harmless, like a gentle little bunny rabbit, completely subdued and harmless. Most of you might even know a Christian and they seem oh so pure and innocent. Let me tell you, they are on the attack! They are destroying the empire from within! From buildings like that one right over there!"

He raised his sword and pointed toward the church. He yelled, "Capture the enemy, torture them, and locate their writings! Enslave their women. Take that building apart, stone by stone! Now, let the war begin!"

Galerius walked over to the other emperors as the trumpet sounded, signaling the beginning of the battle and the start of the purge. Knowing that all four emperors were watching from the balcony, the solders performed with unbridled passion.

The army thundered up the hill. When they arrived before the church, they assumed their attack formation with shields configured to protect their advance. The Christian women wept from a distance as Marcellus was arrested. Huge horses were tied to the columns of the church, pulling down the structure with great force.

Galerius yelled, "Where is your God now!" smiling as he glanced at the other emperors. Constantine stood with his father. The two looked at each other with disgust. Galerius turned his head and noticed their lack of enthusiasm as he glared at them with anger.

That night Constantine was sleeping in his bed in Diocletian's palace. Suddenly, he was awakened as lightning struck and violently shook the building. People scrambled in fear as word spread of a fire. Constantine looked for his mother to make sure she was safe. (7) He found her outside, holding onto her maid as the pouring rain extinguished the fire.

She said to Constantine, "This is God's way of speaking to us. What happened today was wrong, so very wrong!"

Constantine didn't respond, but he thought it was strange that lightning hit the palace the very night the persecution had begun. "Was it God? He thought, "Was there just one God?"

The next day, the new edict was placed on government buildings, starting with Nicaea, and then throughout the entire Roman Empire.

The Edict Against the Christians:

> **I Diocletian, having made it my goal to enhance the republic, have decided that the places of Christian worship should be destroyed, their scriptures eliminated by fire, those who hold positions of honor degraded. And those people, if they persist in their Christian profession, shall be deprived of all liberty.**
>
> **The Edict is drafted on this day of February 23rd in Nicaea (8).**

The Christians were struck with terror when they saw the edict.

Galerius' advisors informed him that there was a large population of Christians in Philadelphia, a few miles to the south of Nicaea. He was also informed that Philadelphia was mentioned in the writings of the Christians as an important city. He immediately left with 25,000 soldiers to enforce the new edict. When he arrived, the residents of Philadelphia saw the army and were put on edge.

Galerius' had an eighteen-year-old nephew named Daza that was being weaned to become an emperor. When they arrived at the

Roman barracks, Daza met privately with one of the Roman officials of Philadelphia.

The official could smell wine on Daza's breath as he asked, "We hear many rumors. What is the reason for your arrival?"

Daza said, "We are here to make certain that the Edict Against the Christians is properly enforced. As you may know, the Christian threat has been growing for some time. Have you read the new edict?"

"Of course, I am required to read all the edicts," said the official, "I'm glad that we are finally taking action."

Well," said Daza, "We are here to squelch the rebellion. As you undoubtedly know, they are everywhere."

Daza paused for a few moments and then continued, "I understand also that there are many beautiful Christian women in this city."

The official smiled and said, "Ah! Oh my! There are many, but there is one more beautiful than any other. We are all haunted by her! Her name is Calista. She hides most of the time. Her husband watches over her constantly. I wouldn't leave my wife alone either if she looked like this woman!"

"Well!" said an excited Daza, "I want you to first capture her husband! After we take care of him, I want you to bring her here to me. If you are successful, I will see to it that you become the tax collector for the entire region. My uncle does everything I ask of him. I will see that you become a very wealthy man in no time, especially if she is as you say."

Practically every Roman soldier in Philadelphia was on the lookout for Antoney. As he was walking along the street, a couple of soldiers recognized him. They quickly approached him from behind and commanded, "By order of the Roman government, you must come now!"

They quickly tied up his arms and then they aggressively walked him through the city. Antoney prayed under his breath as he tried to maintain his composure.

They entered the soldier's barracks and then into the torture area in the courtyard. The two soldiers hyperextended his arms, tying his hands in between two poles.

"What is happening?" demanded Antoney.

The soldiers were silent, looking at him with disdain.

Daza entered the area, drinking his large cup of wine. He smiled from ear to ear and said, "So nice to meet you! You must be Antoney! I've heard much about you! I am Daza, the nephew of the great emperor, Galerius."

Antoney looked at Daza with confusion. Daza was very short and looked like a teenager. He didn't look like a true official for the empire.

Daza said, "Everyone within the Roman Empire is required to worship our supreme emperor Diocletian or face torture and death. You must now pray to the holy emperor and curse Christ."

Daza walked right up to Antoney's face, who could smell the strong pungent scent of alcohol coming from the pores of Daza.

Are you willing?" asked Daza, grinning with delight in his power.

Daza turned and asked one of his men to position a little shrine on a tray in front of Antoney. On the tray was a small statue of Diocletian and a cup of wine.

The War

"Pray to Diocletian now or else!" demanded Daza.

Antoney looked at the little shrine and boldly said, "No, never."

Daza responded, "The laws are very clear and are now finally being enforced. We're putting a stop to your rebellion. Are you willing to offer a sacrifice? If not, then that means I get to have a little fun!"

Daza then said, "I have heard that you have a beautiful wife."

Antoney forced himself to be silent.

Daza said, "And you know what Antoney? I think that I will personally enslave her. She will be mine!"

"No, she won't" said Antoney with confidence as he investigated Daza's black eyes.

Daza said, "You Christians cannot just do as you please! You will never defeat Rome!"

"You cannot do as you please!" exclaimed Antoney. The words seemed to flow out of him. He possessed a boldness that was completely unnerving to Daza.

Daza responded, "Are you telling me what to do? Do you know that I have your destiny in the palm of my hand?"

"No, you don't," said Antoney, "My destiny is determined by God. You my friend, are choosing your destiny right now!"

"Be quiet!" yelled Daza. "You are all a bunch of lying hypocrites!"

Daza began to whip Antoney in the back, taking pleasure in each lash. Antoney gritted his teeth as he suppressed his screams.

Daza went to Antoney's face and said, "If you just say, 'I renounce the Christian God and I worship you Diocletian my emperor, the holy one,' I will let you go free as a bird. None of your friends will know what you did, and you can go home to your wife. It will be our little secret. You will be a free man. Otherwise, you will be tortured to death...slowly and painfully ... and I'll capture your wife and she will be mine!"

Daza went over to his table and poured himself more to drink. He then said, "Worship the emperor?"

Antoney looked down at the image and yelled with all his might, "Never!"

"Sacrifice!" said Daza.

"No!" exclaimed Antoney.

"I'll let you think about it," said Daza.

Antoney exclaimed, "There is nothing to think about!"

"Why? Why? Why are you Christians so foolish?" asked Daza, looking up into the air while maintaining his smirk. He then put down his wine and ran over to Antoney and started viciously whipping him in the back seven times, before pausing.

Antoney exclaimed, "The God who created you is calling you right now! You can have heaven, or you can have hell! The choice is yours. Heaven or hell!"

Daza sat down and stared at the wall. Suddenly, he began to think about his life misery as he sensed truth coming from Antoney.

If he became a Christian, he would lose all the opportunity for pleasure that awaited him. He had great expectations of more money and sex, especially as they confiscated the possessions of the Christians and enslaved their women. He thought, 'What if Antoney's wife is as beautiful as they say? I must have her."

At this moment, Galerius entered the room. Daza began to perform for fear of looking too soft in front of his uncle.

Daza yelled at Antoney, "Where do you keep the writings of the Christians?" glancing at his uncle to see his reaction and make sure he was gaining his approval. Antoney remained silent.

"Tell me where they are!" screamed Daza, as he glanced again at his uncle. "I know that you know where they keep them!"

Galerius walked over to Daza and asked, "Daza, why are you wasting your time?"

He replied, "We're making progress."

Galerius said, "No you aren't! Put him on the rack stretcher!"

They wheeled the dreaded device underneath Antoney. After fastening his arms and legs, the operator slowly turned the wheel, painfully pulling apart Antoney's body. He began to scream, but then the peace of God came upon him. He continued to stare at Daza as the tension continued to get tighter and tighter. Antoney turned to look at Galerius as he withstood the pain. The horrible sound of his joints being torn apart could be heard by all the guards in the courtyard.

"Where do you keep the writings?" yelled Daza.

Galerius interrupted Daza and said firmly" Just kill him. We don't have time for this!" Galerius then yelled at the top of his lungs, "If he isn't going to tell us where the writings are, just kill him!"

Daza then turned to one of his guards and said silently, "Prepare him for the pole. Also, go find his girl and bring her back to me. I want every man available on this!"

Then Antoney was brought outside the barracks.

ADDITIONAL PICTURE:

Daza, Shakko, CC

CHAPTER 5

FLEE!

Church Pillars, Ancient Philadelphia, Simon Jenkins, CC

Sasa was home around midday when she heard someone knock. After opening the door, she was greeted by a strikingly handsome man with brilliantly colored clothes.

He stepped inside and said to her, "Listen to me Sasa! Flee!" He then put his hand up to his mouth and signaled her to be quiet and whispered, "Soldiers are on their way, and you must leave now. Go to Cappadocia. Take your family and your friend Calista and go. Calista will put up a fight, but make sure she goes with you. Don't wait for her husband and don't take anything with you. Flee!"

He then mysteriously walked away.

Sasa's husband was working on their roof with a friend. Sasa grabbed her daughter and ran outside and yelled frantically, "Val! Val! Get down right now! Now!"

When he saw her hysteria, he climbed down as she screamed, "I just spoke to an angel! I'll tell you later!" She grabbed his hand while holding onto their two-year-old daughter. The three ran across the street and barged into Calista's house.

Sasa screamed, "Calista, we need to leave right now!"

Calista asked, "Why? What is happening?"

"We must leave right now!" exclaimed Sasa, "Don't ask questions! There's just no time to talk!"

They ran down an alley into another friend's house as the little girl began to cry hysterically. Soldiers arrived at Calista's house on horseback, looking for her, minutes after the three left.

Meanwhile, Antoney was placed at the center of town, amazed that he wasn't feeling pain after the brutal beating and torture. A soldier painted black sticky tar onto his body with a large brush. They tied his hands and feet to a large pole and then placed the pole in a hole, suspending Antoney about eight feet in the air.

People passing by were curious when they saw that an execution was about to take place. Antoney was highly respected in town and practically everyone recognized him. They couldn't believe that he had committed a crime worthy of death.

He saw familiar faces, while people were asking, "What did he do?"

The soldiers placed a sign on top of the pole that read, "I am a Christian."

A government official walked up to the area in front of Antoney and announced, "This man is guilty of rebellion. He is a Christian. He refuses to bow before our mighty emperor and incites rebellion among the people!"

Several of the officials were instructed beforehand to sneer at him and yell, "Away with him!" They performed as instructed.

Many had heard rumors about the new edict, but nobody was aware of the severity of the punishment. There were several believers present that fearfully walked away.

Galerius said to one of his men, "Go light him on fire." The soldier grabbed a torch that was burning a few feet away from Antoney.

Antoney watched as the man touched his feet with the flame, slowly igniting his body. He felt warmth from the fire, but he felt no pain. He yelled out as loud as he could, "Father, forgive them!"

Seeing flames and black smoke enveloping his sight, he watched the crowd until all was dark. Suddenly he could see again through the black smoke as his body slowly began to float upward toward the sky. He knew exactly what was happening. He looked down at the soldiers and the crowd. As he ascended upward, he began to experience excitement and peace.

A friend arrived at the house where the four were waiting and delivered the news about Antoney. After informing them of the execution, he said, "I know it's horrible, but word is out that they are looking for you Calista. All of you need to flee now!"

Sasa then grabbed Calista as Val embraced his daughter. They quickly ran out the door to a secret tunnel to avoid the main city gates.

After they exited the city, they cautiously walked along the main road to the East and soon found a group of older Jewish traders from Greece. It happened that they were traveling through Cappadocia. Val asked them if they could all travel together and they agreed. After several hours, they stopped to set up their camp. They made a fire, and all stood together warming themselves. Sasa quietly held Calista.

Sasa said, "God is carrying you. He is carrying all of us."

Val shared Calista's story with the Jewish men. Being Jewish, they had also experienced much grief at the hands of the Romans. They were therefore extremely compassionate.

In Israel, in a city called Caesarea along the blue waters of the Mediterranean Sea, there was a special library that was started fifty years before by a man named Origen. Origen traveled throughout the Roman world gathering original Christian writings from every place. He then started a central Christian library in Caesarea. Believers would travel from all over to receive precise copies of the scriptures and other Christian writings. The library employed a team of passionate women that worked around the clock, copying the books (10).

Phillip, the curator of the library, received word of coming persecution. Immediately, he began making plans to transport the most precious writings to Cappadocia. They were sent off in the reliable hands of the women so that the copying could continue. Included in their treasury was a copy of the book of Matthew that was transcribed by the Apostle himself from his original manuscript.

Phillip sent them on their way, but before they left, they all assembled in a circle and prayed earnestly while lifting their hands.

Back at Cappadocia, a man named Artemis walked by one of the government buildings at the center of town. A small crowd had assembled in front of the courtroom with eyes glued on a newly posted edict. Out of curiosity, Artemis walked up and began to read, 'The Edict Against the Christians.'

"This is ridiculous!" He yelled out while turning around to look at the bystanders. "They can't do this!"

He grabbed the sign from its post and tossed it on the ground, and then walked away. A few moments later, a Roman official ran up to him with a couple of soldiers and said, "Did you just pull down that sign!" (11)

"Yes, that's right!" he defiantly replied.

The official commanded the soldiers to bring him into the barracks for questioning. Immediately they chained him to a pole.

"So let me understand something?" said the Roman Official, "Do you think you can just pull down a Roman Edict from its visible position?"

"Yes!" said Artemis confidently, "When it is as ridiculous as the edict I just read."

The official signaled to one of the soldiers. The soldier then walked over to Artemis and struck him in the face. They then placed a little shrine on a tray in front of him.

The official then exclaimed, "You shall die according to the wishes of the Supreme emperor! Unless you are willing to worship Diocletian and offer sacrifice, we are ordered to take dramatic immediate action!"

Artemis stared at the image and yelled, "Never!"

They began to ask him questions about his property and work. After one of the officials spoke with one of the influential people in the area, they determined that he owned some land. He created a quick court session and found Artemis guilty. Without hesitation, they immediately painted his body with tar and erected him into the air at the center of town on a pole. They placed a sign underneath him that read, "I am a Christian." One of the soldiers took a torch and placed it under his feet. The flames quickly enveloped his body as screams were heard throughout the street, terrifying the Christians.

Afterwards, Roman officials immediately went to his home and confiscated his property and then enslaved his wife and children.

Ozgur had picked up some supplies from a nearby farm when he was informed of the persecution. Immediately he ran back to The City of Refuge, arriving just as Daniel was unloading rocks. Ozgur was panting as he said, "Daniel! They just killed Artemis! They are destroying all the churches throughout the empire and killing Christians everywhere!"

A strange clarity came over Daniel at this moment. He boldly said, "We must secure ourselves immediately."

Ozgur said, "I'm going back to town to get my parents!"

"Go!" said Daniel.

All the Christian relatives of the residents quickly went to the City of Refuge. Daniel then had someone secretly contact Nicolas. The two men organized a meeting at a secret cave with 12 other church leaders.

After opening in prayer, Nicolas commenced the meeting by saying, "Brothers, we must develop a plan. We need to work together and coordinate an effort. You might be aware of the City of Refuge. Daniel and his friends have created a phenomenal place. It was as if Daniel knew tragedy was lurking close by! They've been expanding and stockpiling supplies. And get this, they even have an underground well!"

Eyes lit up at the mention of the well.

Daniel said, "The relationships are in place for people to provide more supplies as needed. Currently, we have enough space for about 300 people. We have about 100 full time residents."

Nicolas said, "Daniel, I must commend you. You are like Noah!"

Daniel responded, "I can't possibly take any credit. Honestly, all glory goes to God. I can assure you that I didn't want to be living in the middle of the desert. If I had my way, we never would have left town."

"This location is perfect!" said Nicolas, "Daniel is willing to offer shelter to any true believer who is in fear of persecution and is willing to work."

Daniel said, "And there is plenty of room for expansion. If more people come, we can expand indefinitely. There is no end to how big we can get."

Nicolas said, "A horseman arrived yesterday. I was informed that Phillip from Caesarea is sending two men and a team of women from his library. They are bringing us their most precious writings. Get this, one of their books is an original copy of Matthew's account of Jesus' life! I want them to stay in your underground cave. I've also gathered all the scriptures in the area from various churches. We need to protect them and keep them safe."

"What an honor," said Daniel, "We will do everything within our power to provide for the people and protect the writings."

Nicolas said, "The Romans are targeting and burning the scriptures! Did you know that there are at least two letters that are mentioned in the writings of Paul that are forever gone! We can't ever let this happen again! Preserving the word of God for the next generation is one of the most important tasks that we can complete! Cappadocia is an area known for travelling, it is the perfect hub to secretly transport the scriptures to the different churches. The women from the library in Caesarea work around the clock copying the word of God. We must provide for them and allow this effort to continue."

One of the other church leaders spoke up, "Daniel, am I correct in stating that it is your plan to have women staying with you underground?"

"In our underground cave," said Daniel passionately, "Yes, we will have women. I will have my wife down there and others will have their wives. What are we supposed to do? Separate them? We will allow other women to live among us, but there will be rules. We all know that the Romans target women. Where are they to go?"

"No!" said the man, "If you have women living with men, I cannot and will not allow anyone to participate!"

"Aren't you being absurd right now?" asked Nicolas.

"There will be adultery!" exclaimed the man, "There will be fornication! Even if a man commits the sin in his heart, he has committed the act and is in danger of the fires of hell! When you put men and women together, there is no way to control the passions that inflame the soul! You are creating a recipe for transgression!"

"This is why we need the Spirit of God," said Nicolas, "Without the Spirit of God, we fail. Only the Holy Spirit can strengthen us to conquer our evil desires. We will pray for strength."

"That is a lie!" yelled the man as he jumped to his feet, "There is only one way to conquer sin and that is for people to gauge out their eyes!"

"Gentleman," said Daniel, "We are starting to argue when we need to prepare. Isn't this what the devil wants?"

The man said, "The devil wants us to fail and fall into sin!"

Daniel looked at the man and said, "You are free to go. Please keep the city a secret."

The man got up along with three other people and quickly left the cave.

One of the other men asked, "What do you possess in the way of weapons in your cave?"

Daniel said, "We really don't have many weapons besides a few swords, a couple of spears and a bow and arrow. The Romans don't know that. We can shoot arrows through the hole in the door or drop spears from above the entryway. If we are attacked, we have sulfur that we use to smoke out the enemy. The smoke will do the trick. We discovered it in the rocks down below! It is as if God put it there for us!"

Nicholas said, "Word might travel to the Romans, and they might try to infiltrate us by planting someone inside. People are going to start arriving from all over the world. We must be careful not to discuss The City of Refuge or any of the other havens with anyone. All it takes is one informant. All it takes is one Judas and we are in trouble. Therefore, we need a way to discern the wheat from the chaff. How do we make sure that the wrong people aren't let in?"

Daniel responded, "I've thought about this. We must have a process to verify everyone that enters. We'll have a cave close by where the travelers can be tested. If they pass, then they will be transported over and be allowed to enter the city."

Nicholas said, "Ah, yes! I know a woman named Angela. She loves God more than anyone I know. She is amazing with people, and she has an incredible gift of discernment, but how will she know that the people who show up are looking for the City of Refuge?"

Daniel interjected, "We'll have the travelers do the Ichthys."

"Of course!" replied Nicolas.

The Ichthys was a 'fish' symbol that Christians all over the world used to tell if a person was a genuine Christian. One made a curving line in the ground, and the other person would complete the shape of the fish. If this was done properly, one could tell that the other person was in fact a believer.

Nicholas continued, "Once we know that a person is a true believer, then and only then will they be brought to The City of Refuge."

Daniel said, "What if we blindfold the people when they come to The City of Refuge from the testing place? That way we aren't disclosing the location. Also, we'll want to only bring people late at night in the dark."

Nicholas said, "Yes, that's a great idea! That way, none of the residents will really know the location. If they are apprehended and tortured, they won't know where it is located. If anyone leaves, they must be blindfolded as well."

Everyone was fearful, but they were encouraged. After they fervently prayed, everyone left and began preparing for the challenges ahead.

CHAPTER 6

ARRIVAL

Cappadocia, Linda M. Caldwell, CC

Traveling from Philadelphia to Cappadocia took the group about a week. The Jewish traders were gracious to share their food. Val wanted to tell them the good news about Jesus, even though he didn't think that they would listen.

He said, "Have you men ever read the book of Isaiah from the Jewish scriptures where it talks about the Messiah?"

"I am zealous for the things of God," said one of the men, "But I have not studied the writings of Isaiah."

Val perked with enthusiasm as he began to recite several of prophecies about Jesus. Sasa prayed earnestly as she listened to their dialogue as they walked along.

After talking for about an hour, they approached a riverbed and stopped. Val boldly explained baptism and asked the men if they would like to receive Jesus and be baptized. All three said yes with enthusiasm. Val couldn't believe it! Despite knowing about the horror of the persecution, they were still willing to decide to receive Christ.

Sasa had a friend named Julia living in the center of Cappadocia. When they all arrived, she and her husband were at home and overjoyed to see everyone. They sat them down and made a huge meal.

Val conveyed the story about his new Jewish friends and how they came to believe. Simon and his wife celebrated as they were deeply encouraged when they heard this. They also shared the story of Antoney and the eruption of persecution.

Simon knew Daniel from church and described the City of Refuge. They immediately decided that this was where they needed to go.

The Jewish travelers departed for India, but before they left, they all prayed together.

Then Julia led the team out of town. After making their way deep into the desert to a small cave, Julia said, "Go speak with the sweet woman that lives over there. Her name is Angela. She runs the 'test' cave. Draw the ichthus to let her know that you are all believers."

They had no idea they were the first new recruits to the City of Refuge. Val knocked on the door as an elderly woman appeared with gentle eyes.

"Can I help you," said the woman.

Val asked, "Are you Angela?"

She stepped outside and replied, "Yes. What can I do for you?"

Arrival

They stared at each other as Val walked over to some dirt and made a curve shape with his finger. He turned to look to see Angela's response. Angela walked over and made another curve to form the shape of a fish in the dirt. The two smiled at each other.

Angela looked at Sasa's daughter and said, "You are just the cutest little girl!"

The girl smiled back as Val held her hand.

Angela began to carefully ask questions, "Where are you people from?"

Sasa answered, "Philadelphia, to the West."

Angela said, "Oh Beautiful city! I've never been there, but I read about Philadelphia. Isn't there a famous author that mentioned Philadelphia in his writings?"

Val said, "Yes, it was mentioned by a man named John."

Angela said, "That's right." She stared at Val in a piercing way and said, "Come inside for a bit and let's have something to drink."

Angela carefully watched each reaction to her simple questions. There were many people that had been Christians at one time but had fallen away. She was looking for something beyond just the right answers. After several minutes, it became obvious to Angela that these people were genuine. Angela sent to have some men come and transport the team. They waited until it was dark and then all four were blindfolded. Then they held the shoulders of the person in front of them, forming a train and were brought to the entrance of The City of Refuge.

As they walked through the door, the little girl said, "Mommy, it smells terrible here. I don't like it."

Angela said, "The smell helps us keep people away. Behind this door is where we keep all the animals and toilets."

Angela took a special stick and pushed it through the hole in the middle of the stone.

Suddenly there was a loud grinding sound as the door shook and slowly began to move. It took at least six people to move the enormous and heavy round stone door.

They removed their blindfolds and saw Daniel, Ozgur and Anasia. Angela gave each one of them a kiss goodbye. The big stone door closed behind her.

Anasia helped the women get situated while Ozgur got acquainted with Val.

For Daniel, the images of Calista taking off her blindfold burned in his mind. For a few seconds, he began to conspire ways in which he could have her. Suddenly, he realized that he was listening to the voice of the devil. He repented and prayed that his eyes would only be for his wife. Later, he shared his struggle with Nicolas, and they prayed for strength and focus on his wife.

The fresh recruits found their place in the city with new quarters and daily responsibilities. Of course, they didn't like it down below, but they appreciated the sense of security and the relationships.

Meanwhile, back at Galerius' palace, he received reports that many of his soldiers were showing compassion towards the Christians. He sought a means to impassion the soldiers for his cause, and so he called for Daza late at night to discuss a plan.

The two sat down as Galerius looked Daza in the eyes and said, "You know that Diocletian will either die or retire soon. When either scenario happens, as you know, I will become the supreme leader of the entire Roman Empire! Your uncle will become the most powerful man in the world!"

Daza shook his head.

"When this happens, you will have the opportunity to rise to prominence and become an emperor! Imagine that Daza! You were just a lonely shepherd a few years ago, and now you could become an emperor of the Roman Empire! Everything you could ever want will be at your fingertips!"

Daza's body began to tingle with excitement.

"We will do away with the other emperors, and it will be just the two of us. However, I demand that you prove your obedience to me. You must not let anyone know what I am about to ask of you."

"Oh, yes. I owe everything to you" said Daza. "I realize that everything that I have is because of you and I would never betray you."

Galerius stared at his nephew for a few moments and said, "I proved myself to Diocletian several years ago. Unlike you, I started as a soldier. Very quickly, I demonstrated my abilities on the battlefield. You have not had to endure the dreadful wars that I experienced. I was under a general as we fought the Persians. Diocletian secretly met with me and told me he wanted me to kill this general. His name is unimportant. I fulfilled his wishes and that is why I have the position I have today. I proved myself faithful."

Galerius was lying to Daza. He killed the general to advance in rank. It had nothing to do with Diocletian.

Daza shook his head.

Well." said Galerius, "I need you to set Diocletian's palace on fire." He paused and then continued, "Perhaps he will die from the fire. Let's hope that happens. Either way, we will circulate word that the Christians did it. Of course, it will make perfect sense that they would retaliate. After you prove yourself faithful, you will be promoted to a position as emperor as soon as Diocletian quits. I sincerely believe that this will be the tipping point for him. The old bag can't last much longer. I will become the supreme emperor and you will work for me."

Daza was nervous, but he got up and left for Nicaea with a letter for Diocletian. After he arrived on horseback with three men, they allowed him and his men to sleep in the palace, as they prepared a letter for him to take back to Galerius.

In the middle of the night, Daza arose from his bed and slipped away to fulfill his mission. Going underneath the huge structure, he created a small fire after pouring oil on a wood beam. He then used his candle to light the fire. He watched the fire spread as excitement caused tingles all over his body. Then he made his way back into his chamber and waited for the sound of commotion. When he heard coughing and screams of terror, he ran out of the palace, pretending to be surprised.

Diocletian was awakened by his attendant screaming. "Sir! The palace is on fire!" (12)

He barely made it out of the door to safety, but within a few minutes, the entire structure was enveloped in flames. A crowd of workers stood in shock as they watched the amazing building crash to the ground.

Still in his sleeping clothes, Diocletian commanded his army to surround the blaze. He feared that he would be attacked and killed at a vulnerable moment. He then moved to a secret underground compartment away from the burning structure until word came to him that all was secure.

Arrival

After surveying the damage a few hours later, one of his officers reported, "The Christians must have infiltrated our staff. They are the only ones that would commit such a crime."

Infuriated, Diocletian commanded everyone to line up in rows. He went down the line looking each person in the eye.

"You did it didn't you!" yelling at the terrified baker, slapping him in the face he as he commanded, "I want this one tortured!" Many were suspected, but nobody confessed despite the pain of the rack and the piercing whip.

After the incident, he decided to move back to Rome.

Diocletian immediately released the Second Edict Against the Christians, demanding house to house searches, forcing residents to worship on the spot or face torture and death.

They rewarded the soldiers with a bonus each time they discovered a Christian, also allowing them to take a percentage of the believer's belongings.

A rogue band of Christians in Cappadocia attacked and killed several Roman soldiers. When word reached Galerius, he once again called Daza into his chamber.

"The Christians have attacked our soldiers in Cappadocia," said Galerius. "I've informed Diocletian. This just proves what I've been saying all along! These monsters are a horrible threat to everything peaceful and good. Take 25,000 troops with you and go to Cappadocia. Destroy the meeting places of the Christians and enslave as many as you can!"

The Underground City of Cappadocia

It took about a week for Daza to arrive in town with his soldiers. The people of Cappadocia stopped their work, stepping outside to see the huge marching army.

Immediately, the soldiers gathered in the attack formation in front of Daniel's old church. Daza asked one of his commanders, "What are we to do with a cave?"

"I don't know sir," stated the commander.

Daza held his large cup of wine in his hand as he commanded his men with a drunken slur, "Let's fill the cave with wood and light it on fire. "

The troops forced some slaves to gather spare wood and move it inside the cave. They ignited the wood and watched it burn as a crowd assembled to witness the inferno.

"I guess that is the best we can do," said Daza as he yelled out loud, "Let this a warning to all of you! Do not have anything to do with any Christians and if you are a Christian, we are coming after you!"

Daza then met Cyprian, the local tax collector. He explained his quest for the writings of the Christians, and then he asked Cyprian if he knew of any beautiful Christian women.

"Ah," said Cyprian, "There were many, but they're all gone."

"What do you mean, they're all gone?'" asked Daza.

"Most of the Christians have disappeared! They have vanished!" said Cyprian, "nobody knows where they are."

"Don't be ridiculous," said Daza, "Where would they go?"

"Some say they have moved to a forest to the East, others believe that they have left earth," said Cyprian.

"They must be somewhere," said Daza, "And we will find them!"

One of the Roman officials apprehended Justin, the pastor of Daniel's old church. He was brought into the barracks where he stood before Daza. Daza didn't say a word or look at the man, but just sipped on his wine. Daza finally got up with his whip in hand.

All the true believers of Cappadocia avoided Justin. His teachings had become self-serving to fulfill his own sexual appetites. Daniel and Nicolas specifically requested that nobody mention the City of Refuge to him.

Daza said loudly, "We must begin the process!"

He turned to Justin, "I hear that you are a leader of the Christians and that you stand in the way of the mighty gods of Rome."

Justin said while panting, "They took the position away from me. I am no longer a leader."

"No longer a leader?" said Daza with a devious smile as he walked around him, playing with the whip and practicing his whipping motion, "Have you renounced the God of the Christians?"

"No," said Justin.

"Well, I'm here to help you," said Daza, as he quickly turned and began to ferociously whip Justin's back four times.

Daza yelled, "I need you to renounce the Christian God and worship the gods of the Roman Empire!"

Justin yelled, "All right, stop! I'll do whatever you want! Please just stop it, please!" as he cried while panting.

Daza was surprised at how quickly he acquiesced and looked at the men around him. "Great!" said Daza. "Look at the image of our emperor and worship him! I want you to get down on your knees, kiss the statue and say, 'I renounce Christ and the God of the Christians. I worship you the true god. I worship you and exalt you.' Ah, it is so simple! Then, I want you to enjoy some wine with your god."

Justin cried as he repeated the words, shaking as he bowed before the image and then he kissed it.

"Now, give me the names of all the Christians in the area!" demanded Daza.

He gave the names of everyone he could remember. On the list were Daniel, Nicolas, Ozgur and several others.

"Which ones are wealthy?" asked Daza.

"This man right here," said Justin, "His name is Gilley. He owns many inns in the area. Perhaps he is the wealthiest man in all of Cappadocia."

"Very nice!" said Daza while smiling, "We also need the writings of the Christians. Do you have any idea where they keep their writings?"

Justin said, "I have some writings at my house that I will gladly hand over to you. The main leader for our area is named Nicolas. He oversees all the churches, and he has many writings, but nobody knows where he is."

Daza said, "Okay, I think you know where this person is hiding!"

"He has disappeared!" said Justin as he shook with fear.

"Get the stretcher machine ready," demanded Daza to his guards.

Justin screamed, "I have no idea where he is! I'll work with you to find him! I'll do anything!"

Daza turned to Justin and said, "These soldiers will be accommodating you to the writings at your home. Don't withhold a single page. I assure you that I won't hesitate to burn your body. If I find out that you have anything else in your possession, I will give you a miserable and painful death."

Justin escorted them to the scriptures he had at home. The next day they publicly burned all the parchments outside the central Roman government building. Some of the Christians still living in town watched as the precious pages went up in flames.

Later that day, Justin walked past the Roman temple and saw the seductive statues of the beautiful vestal virgins. He stopped and stared. He was now free to pursue pleasure. His mind rejoiced that he could do whatever he wanted. All his life he had heard stories about the sexual interactions of the priests with the so called "vestal virgins." He was able to meet with some of the priests to see what was involved in becoming one of them. The priests loved the idea of having a so called, 'Christian convert,' working with them.

Daza's soldiers went to the center of town, setting up stations where they would ask people if they had seen those on the list. They offered money and tax breaks to anyone willing to give information that would lead to an arrest.

Justin began to tell the Christians that weren't hiding, "God understands and wants us to avoid needless suffering. Worship the emperor. It's no big deal. It is our responsibility as citizens to worship him."

This teaching spread as many other church leaders started following Justin's lead.

Daza had seen a beautiful 17-year-old girl working at her family's clothing shop in the Market District. He said to one of his soldiers, "I want you to see if she might be a Christian."

The soldiers approached her as she stood with her assortment of clothes. Some of the clothing was created in The City of Refuge.

"What is your name?" said one of the soldiers.

She fearfully answered, "My name is Adara."

"Come with me to worship the emperor," said the soldier.

Adara replied, "I can't because I'm the only one watching the family shop."

The soldier turned his head and approached some of the other merchants. He asked a woman "Do you know if that girl over there named Adara is one of the Christians?"

"Oh yes she is," the other merchant said, "She and her entire family. I know it for a fact." The woman was a competitor. She despised the girl and her family because they gave people more value and therefore had more business.

"If you can tell us where she lives, you and your family won't have to pay taxes for the rest of the year," said the Roman soldier.

The woman happily agreed to give the information. She stopped her work and went with the soldiers to the street and pointed to the house.

That next morning, Adara was getting ready to go to work when she heard a loud knock. She reluctantly opened the door and saw two large Roman soldiers towering above her. One of them commanded, "You are required to come with us for questioning."

Adara thought for a second, fully aware of what was about to happen. If she went with them, she would be enslaved and raped endlessly by the Roman soldiers.

The Romans had ruthlessly raped one of her friends. The images of her friend in a crying rage and then falling into a catatonic state were unbearable. Adara knew that it would be much worse for her. Christians were being raped until they were dead by an endless number of soldiers.

"Can I first just grab some things out of my bedroom," she said.

"Be quick," they replied.

She went into her room and pulled out a knife and said with a cry, "Lord, please take me!"

The soldiers heard a loud thump. When they opened the door to her room, they saw her bloody body lying on the floor.

(*Authors Note: The story was recorded by the Historian Eusubius during the Great Persecution. Suicide is never the solution. However, this situation highlights the horror of the persecution)

They went back to Daza and informed him of what had happened.

He said, "Shame. What a waste. Well, I found some other amazing women around town. This city is crawling with them!"

CHAPTER 7

NEW RECRUITS

Underground City Door, Walkwa, Nevit, CC

One evening, a 24-year-old man named Stephen from Ephesus arrived with two other people. He came from a lineage of wealthy Christians. When the persecution started, the Romans killed his father and brothers so they could confiscate the family's property. The Christians of Ephesus hid Stephen away in the local mountains, but eventually they sent him to Cappadocia with some precious documents.

"I heard that you are copying the scriptures," said Stephen after he was introduced to Daniel.

Daniel said, "Yes. The Romans have been relentless in their goal of destroying the word of God. We have over 60 people that are working as much as they can to make precise copies."

Stephen said, "I have something very special to show you."

Stephen handed Daniel a leather case. Daniel carefully pulled out some deteriorating parchments.

Stephen explained, "That is the Apostle Paul's original letter to the Ephesians. My father kept it in a secret vault. When I left for Cappadocia, the believers insisted that I bring this with me and deliver it to you people."

"This is incredible!" said Daniel as he marveled at the brittle pages in his hands. He noticed the segment at the end that was personally signed by the Apostle Paul.

Although Stephen grew up in a Christian family, he was constantly sleeping with different women, drinking, and involved in shady business deals. His family's beliefs were more of a deficit to him than anything else. If not for family pressure, he would have worshiped Diocletian's image long ago. He came to Cappadocia for his personal safety and that was it.

The persecution continued to rage as the Romans enjoyed easy plunder. The numbers at The City of Refuge continued to grow. Christian slaves started arriving in large numbers, as word spread that they could find safety.

Slaves that had escaped and were recaptured, were immediately crucified by the empire. The Romans also gave a reward to anyone giving information that would lead to a slave's recapture. For the slaves branded with the word 'fugitive,' there was little chance that they could survive. Daniel was overjoyed that he could help and celebrated the arrival of every Christian slave.

A short time later, Daza was called to another region. The Christians were relieved when word reached their ears that he was gone.

The Underground City of Cappadocia

The Romans released "The Third Edict Against the Christians," which called for large scale worship of the emperor throughout the Roman Empire. Public gatherings could be forced at any time, and all those unwilling to worship were to be killed on the spot.

Shortly after the release of the new edict, a couple was brought into The City of Refuge. When Daniel heard their story, he asked them to speak to the entire group at their evening meeting.

Daniel started the service with a prayer and then said, "I want to introduce a couple from Hierapolis."

Hierapolis was 50 miles west of Cappadocia.

"This is Simon and Sien. As many of you know, the Romans have released a new edict calling for deeper persecution. I'm going to allow them to tell their story. Come up please," said Daniel.

Sien forced herself to speak despite her anguish. She said, "As many of you know, Hierapolis had an incredible community of believers. I say had! A couple of weeks ago, the Roman officials called everyone in Hierapolis into the center of the city. They had positioned large logs behind the people. About nine hundred adults and children were standing around, confused while waiting. We just happened to be on our way back into town when the roundup happened, so we watched from a hill in the distance. The Roman soldiers surrounded everyone with swords and torches. They began to march toward the people while lighting the logs on fire in the center, forcing everyone into the flames! People were either burned or sliced to pieces. Afterwards, they burned all the bodies right there at the center of town!"

Her husband took over as he held her, "The horror of the images in our minds are tormenting us. Some friends in town led us to you people."

Many in the meeting started crying as Daniel and Anasia approached the couple and held them.

In the following months, new recruits to The City of Refuge brought stories of inconceivable brutality. Children were reporting their parents to the authorities. Parents turned their own children over for believing in Jesus. Christians became distrustful of each other and feared meeting in any setting. The Romans were feeding Christians to the lions in the arenas throughout the Roman Empire, while others had their eyes gouged out and were sent to the mines.

There was no boundary to the level of cruelty exhibited by the Romans. They were so diligent in their efforts to go after the Christians, they released all the criminals in prison to create room for them. The crime rate exploded because of the thugs on the streets, as life became more miserable for everyone. The empire blamed the spike in crime on the Christians, issuing false reports as another means to continue to justify and increase the persecution.

Living underground became more difficult: the men were forced to chisel and transport rocks to make room for more residents. Food shortages, darkness and the ever-present fear of the Romans made life almost unbearable. Fortunately, the Lord's presence was with the people. Everyone talked about the sense of peace and joy they were experiencing amidst the challenges. In their meetings, they would sing songs to the Lord and afterwards, they walked away feeling refreshed.

Each night, several people were allowed outside to transport the feces from the toilets to the areas where they were growing crops. It was a precious time despite the wretched smells. When they were finished, they would all come together in a circle to sing a song to the Lord and look at the stars while enjoying the fresh air.

One evening, Daniel was forced to face the ultimate trial. Things were already tough for him, but Daniel was about to face his life's greatest challenge.

He was in the middle of a task when he was told that some new recruits had just arrived and were waiting to be let in. He stopped what he was doing and approached the stone door with Ozgur. Angela greeted him through the hole.

"Daniel," she said, "There are four men here and two of them say that they know you."

He was excited when he saw the tool-shop owner, but when he saw the person next to him, his heart dropped. Ozgur observed Daniel turn around with his back to the door and slide to the floor while holding his head.

"Let me talk to him!" demanded Gilley, looking into the hole. He begged while smiling, "Daniel, my good friend! The Romans took everything from me! I barely escaped! They are after me and I can't go back to town or anywhere! You are my only hope!"

Daniel got up and then stepped back and said, "Oh Lord! No! Why? Why?"

He turned around and yelled through the hole, "No! Never! There are other places for you!"

"What's wrong?" inquired Ozgur.

Daniel glanced at Ozgur and said, "Go ahead and look!"

Ozgur peaked through the hole and then turned to Daniel and said, "No!" shaking his head.

Gilley pleaded through the hole, "Daniel, you have to help me! The Romans are hunting me down! There are many soldiers torturing everyone to get information! They are specifically looking for me!"

Daniel said, "Good! You'll finally get what you deserve!"

Daniel remembered the scripture from the book of Romans that he read earlier that day:

> **'If your enemy is hungry, feed him; if he is thirsty, give him something to drink. In doing this, you will heap burning coals on his head. Do not be overcome by evil but overcome evil with good.'**
>
> **-Romans 12:20**

"Why did I have to read that today?" he said to himself.

Daniel knew that if he were to let Gilley in, he would try to take control and conspire against him. It was his nature to do anything in his power to take control. The men who were already a challenge would align with Gilley and he would be in for a fight.

"Gilley, I do not want you in here! It is tough enough! Now I beg you, just go away!"

"Daniel! I cannot go anywhere!" bellowed Gilley with tears, "I did not know you were here! If we get out of this mess, you can have your house back free and clear. I will give you the Inn also. Daniel, I am sorry. Please forgive me!"

Daniel wanted to throw some harsh words at Gilley as he stared at Ozgur.

Daniel said to Ozgur, "I don't want him here."

"You can't just turn him away?" said Ozgur.

"Ahhh!" said Daniel, speaking through the door to Gilley, "If I let you in, you must follow our rules. Do you hear me?"

"Yes Daniel. I promise!"

They opened the door as Daniel greeted the shop-owner and then looked at Gilley. Gilley towered over Daniel and Ozgur. With his long extra thick beard and muscular strong arms, he made the men feel insecure for a moment.

"Who are these?" asked Daniel when he saw a couple of men behind Gilley.

"They are my slaves. Good Christian slaves," said Gilley.

Daniel said, "There are no slaves in here."

"Why not Daniel?" said Gilley, "Why don't you allow slaves? Slaves are people too."

"Precisely, if they come in, these men immediately become your equal and they are permanently free."

Gilley said, "No Daniel!"

Daniel said, "Then go somewhere else! I am not bargaining with you! It's a different world down here."

"Alright," said Gilley as he forced himself to acquiesce, "I'll let them go."

"Permanently," required Daniel.

"Alright," muttered Gilley, expressing obvious resistance.

The two men rejoiced as Daniel introduced himself to them.

Gilley then looked at the two men and commanded, "Grab the bags."

"Wait! This isn't an Inn Gilley," said Daniel, "You cannot have that much stuff down here. Also, you don't get to tell them what to do. Do you understand? They are not your slaves anymore. They are free. You get to bring in one bag," as he smiled at the two men.

Gilley said, "I've got money and a lot of important things."

Daniel replied, "Good. Give us all your money. That is the price of getting in. Everyone who comes here gives us all their money. We will need it to buy supplies and you can only bring one bag. We are all just surviving. Give your extra belongings to Angela and she will sell them in town and bring us the cash."

Gilley looked at Daniel and thought about the alternative… torture and death.

"Whatever you say Daniel," said Gilley.

When Anasia found out that Gilley had entered the city, she was infuriated.

CHAPTER 8

A NEW SUPREME EMPEROR

Galerius, CC

305AD

TWO YEARS AFTER THE START OF THE PERSECUTION

Since the time the persecution started, Diocletian's health deteriorated quickly. His chronic stomach pain was intolerable and he started experience panic attacks. After lying in bed for ten straight days, he called in his top advisor.

"I'm finished!" Diocletian exclaimed, "I want out! I am no longer fit, nor do I want to be the supreme emperor or any kind of emperor. I no longer have the strength to play this game!"

"Sir," said the advisor, "You have done so much good for the empire. Whom, might I ask, have you chosen to succeed you?"

A New Supreme Emperor

Diocletian stated, "I want Constantius to abandon his region and take my position as the supreme emperor."

The advisor said, "If you do this your eminence, Galerius and his men will undoubtedly revolt against the other emperors and there will be a bloody civil war. You have but one choice if you want to avoid war. Unfortunately, you must choose Galerius if you are to maintain peace and semblance."

Diocletian said, "The man is a barbarian!"

He thought about the wisdom of his advisor and the consequences of choosing someone else and then said, "Galerius shall become the supreme emperor because I do not have any more fight in me. What if we have Constantine become a junior emperor under Galerius?"

"Your eminence," said the advisor, "A person like Galerius will not accept Constantine. Pay attention. He will see him as a threat and try to kill him through assassination or war."

"Well," said Diocletian, "I am the supreme emperor, and I will decide."

"It is your choice your eminence," said the advisor.

A few weeks later, all the emperors and top officials were ordered to meet in Thessaloniki in Greece to inaugurate Galerius as the supreme emperor. When Diocletian arrived the night before the ceremony, he was greeted by a drunken Galerius in his palace. Galerius had just erected a huge statue of himself in his courtyard and was eager for Diocletian to see it. They walked outside the door and were suddenly dwarfed by a giant marble Galerius.

Galerius pointed to the statue and proudly said, "So what do you think Diocletian?"

He said, "I don't want to look at your statue."

Galerius pretended not to hear Diocletian as he stared at the huge stone image of himself, "I've gone through six sculptors. It was finished by a 17-year-old. The kid is a complete prodigy, a genius! Come on Diocletian, you must agree! Admit that it is amazing!"

Diocletian was looking down at the ground, avoiding Galerius. He then said, "Galerius! I am obviously done with the empire. I do not want any part of it anymore. When I retire, I want to be finished. Please do not disturb me and do not cause friction with the other emperors."

"Yes," said Galerius, "I will not disturb you. Everyone believes the empire will be much better off without you."

"No Galerius," said Diocletian, "Men like you think of only one person! You will prop up your band of thieves as they do your bidding. Everybody else will suffer! You will pretend to promise the world, but once you are in control, you will only benefit yourself!

"Oh no, look at you Diocletian," responded Galerius, "Weak and pathetic! As if you ever thought of anyone other than yourself!"

"I'm not going to respond," said Diocletian looking at the ground, "I do have just one thing to ask of you."

"And what is that?" inquired Galerius.

"Don't fight the other emperors until I'm dead," demanded Diocletian.

Galerius responded, "I just have one thing to ask of you."

"And what is that?" asked Diocletian.

A New Supreme Emperor

Galerius said, "Constantine's father is sympathetic to the Christians. He has not been fulfilling his obligation to stop the menacing force. As you know, Christians are fleeing to France, and he is dividing the Roman Empire. Some are saying that he may be a Christian! I will have to invade unless you help me."

"So, what do you propose?" asked Diocletian.

"I do not want Constantine replacing me as a junior emperor. He cannot take my position," said Galerius. "There is no doubt that he will also side with the Christians. Then we will have three safe Christian harbors since I am already having a tough time with Maxentius."

Maxentius was Galerius' son-in-law and the emperor of Italy and Spain.

Galerius continued, "Maxentius is an idiot! Christians are enjoying complete freedom under his rule!"

"Ok, I know what is coming. Whom have you chosen?" asked Diocletian.

"I want Daza," said Galerius.

"Oh no!" exclaimed Diocletian, "Constantine has been reared since his youth to be an emperor! He has proven himself a dignified warrior! He is highly educated, incredibly intelligent, and everyone respects him! Daza is a weak drunkard and has absolutely no business becoming an emperor!"

Galerius said, "He does whatever I tell him to do."

"That is the only reason you want him. There will be a revolt! Look! Already you are being a fool!"

After delivering these words, Diocletian was silent for a moment as he felt stress and sickness moving over his body. He calmed himself down and refocused on his goal of exiting the empire.

He said, "You know what Galerius, I will do whatever you want! After I am finished, please just leave me alone. I beg you! Leave me alone!"

"Good," said Galerius, "Daza and I will work together."

"Yes, you two will work together to ruin everything for everybody!" yelled Diocletian. "I can see destruction on the horizon! Everybody will suffer just because of one greedy idiot!"

Diocletian turned and walked away to his quarters followed by three guards as Galerius considered killing him.

The next day, the two emperors waited for the carriage to arrive but said nothing to each other. When it pulled up, they entered. They sat across from each other but did not utter a word.

Hundreds of governors and other officials flocked from all over the empire for the inauguration. When Diocletian and Galerius exited the carriage, Diocletian remained silent, although many people approached him wanting his attention, he had nothing to say.

Constantine was waiting, supposing that he would be greeted, but he was shunned by all. When he approached Diocletian, he was met by a guard pushing him away. Galerius and Daza would periodically glance at him, knowing that he was in for a little surprise.

All those seeking position within the Roman Empire were attempting to flatter Galerius. They fished for any way to get close to him. He was the gateway to power.

A New Supreme Emperor

After the trumpet sounded, the crowd entered Galerius' new temple for the very first time. All were mesmerized by the design. The Romans had discovered concrete and were making incredible buildings with this new material. All in attendance were fascinated with the huge dome. It was perfectly round, without a single visible groove. This had never been possible in the past, but now the inconceivable was achievable.

The ceremony began as the beautiful vestal virgins slowly entered the building, making their trademark seductive movements. Never had there been such an assemblage of physically perfect women. Galerius had appointed 12 men to travel throughout the entire Roman Empire to select the twelve most alluring vestal virgins just for this event.

The building, the virgins, the powerful people, invigorated Galerius, making him feel invincible. All those in attendance were bewildered by the glory of the moment.

The virgins bowed down before the new Supreme emperor and covered his feet with their white powder, smiling playfully as they worshipped him, performing their dance. Galerius slowly nodded his head in agreement as he stared at each of them from head to toe.

The reality of Galerius' position as the most powerful man in the world hit him like a bolt of lightning. His heart began to beat uncontrollably. He thought of conquering Persia, Germany, India and surpassing all the triumphs of Alexander the Great. History would see him as the greatest ever!

The high priest signaled Diocletian to come forward. He walked toward Galerius and removed his crown. Then he heartlessly placed it on the new supreme emperor. Another priest stepped forward with a new purple robe adorned with golden stripes and they placed it on Galerius' large body. Then they removed Diocletian's robe.

Diocletian said, "I present the new supreme emperor of the Roman Empire."

The crowd cheered.

Diocletian continued; Galerius' position as junior emperor will be filled by."

He paused as he looked down in disgust and mumbled, "Daza."

Everyone gasped in horror as they looked at each other in utter disbelief. Several people said to each other, "Did he just say Daza?"

Diocletian ignored the crowd as he slowly walked away for the last time, seeking to avoid any conversation. He thought of one thing, escaping the people that were making his existence so miserable. The faster he could get away, the better. He didn't want to answer any questions about Daza.

Daza gazed at Constantine with a sinister grin.

The crowd turned to Constantine to see his reaction. Constantine whispered to his friend, "Let's get out of here quick," as he smiled at the multitude. The two fearfully slipped out of the building, making their way past the gates of Thessaloniki on horseback.

A new purple toga was placed on Daza as everyone watched with bewildered amusement. All the priests and the other emperors concluded the ceremony by gathering around a lamb.

The high priest yelled at the top his lungs, staring at Galerius in the eyes, "To the great emperor Galerius! You and only you are worthy to receive this sacrifice! You are worthy of our worship. You are a god!"

The priest walked forward and then bowed down before Galerius. After rising, he guided Galerius' hand on the head of the lamb. The other emperors surrounded him as the animal began to struggle and squirm. The priest pulled out a blade and slowly slit the lamb's throat as blood gushed onto the ground. Galerius smiled, and then looked at the other emperors.

The priest looked at Galerius and said, "You are not a man, you are a god! Permit us to bow down before you now!"

He shook his head in agreement as everyone in the room fell on their knees while Galerius looked around the temple.

After the ceremony, the crowd walked a short distance to Galerius' victory arch. On horseback, he unsheathed his sword and raised it high above his head. Traveling through the newly created arch, the crowd exploded. In the courtyard before the arch, they began their celebration with a feast.

Galerius demanded that he have his own table and be left alone with Daza. All the officials wanted to sit with Galerius, but he refused them all.

He did not have to appease, compliment, or prove anything. It was now the responsibility of all the world to please him. Each time he rejected a governor or official, it gave him a sense of pleasure and reminded him of his position of power. Only four beautiful women were allowed to join him and Daza, even Galerius' wife was denied the opportunity. The young women sat silently, smiling at each other as the two men glanced at them periodically.

It was against the rules of the empire for anyone to sleep with a vestal virgin, but that night Galerius and Daza took their pick of women from ceremony as the two engaged in a drunken orgy.

When Galerius awoke with a hangover, he looked at the two young women lying next to him. He got up and spoke with his guard and demanded, "Get them out of here now!"

The women were escorted out of the room and led back to their group of fellow virgins. It felt pleasant for Galerius to treat beautiful women poorly. All the world esteemed and worshiped these women, but he could use and abuse them.

Galerius then prepared himself and called for his top official. When he arrived, he said, "I want to release a fourth edict against the Christians. It must state that all within the empire must publicly worship the emperor or face death, even the young children. Yes! Why should they not worship me? Also, we must double the number of temples throughout the empire." (12)

The official replied with a sense of sarcasm, "Hm…That is a great idea sir, and we will get on it immediately. However, how is it that we shall pay for this project?"

Galerius said, "We'll start taxing the people in Rome. We will finally get money from those idiots. It is about time they paid. I also understand that we are flush with Christian slave labor with more on the way! I love the idea of seeing Christians working on our temples."

The commander said, "Certainly sir. We will start the process immediately."

He walked away rolling his eyes because it was a ridiculous request. The Roman Empire didn't have the money to double the number of temples. He was asking for the most monumental project in 850 years of Roman history. Nonetheless, the commander proceeded to begin the effort.

A New Supreme Emperor

Galerius had given his only daughter to Maxentius, the junior emperor ruling over Italy and Spain. Before Maxentius went home to Rome, he quickly met with Galerius.

After some small talk, Galerius got down to business with Maxentius. He demanded, "You must start taxing the people of Italy. We are doubling the number of temples within the empire, and we need the revenue. If the empire is to survive, we need to support the power that has brought us so much prosperity. It is not fair that your people do not pay taxes while the rest of the world carries the burden! This is dividing the empire! You had a free ride before, but not anymore!"

The people of Italy believed that they were immune from taxation. The Roman Empire started with them, and it was called the Roman Empire. Yet not one of the current emperors were from Rome, or Italy for that matter. Diocletian had moved the center of power to Nicaea, partly to justify taxation on the people of Italy.

Maxentius appeased his father-in-law by saying, "I'll discuss the matter as soon as I get to Rome," with an unconvincing blank look.

He knew that there would be a revolt if he ever tried to tax the people and so did Galerius. It was all a ploy by Galerius to justify an invasion (13). If he manipulated the people to rebel because of taxation, that would justify his desire to attack Rome with an powerful large army. He could then rule the area and do away with Maxentius.

Maxentius didn't trust Galerius. His wife, Galerius' own daughter, dreaded her father and was constantly warning her husband about his manipulative ways.

Galerius went on, "I hear also that Rome is rampant with Christian rats living in holes. You must follow the edicts and destroy the Christians! Your area is becoming a safe harbor! We must be united on this issue, otherwise, the Christians will take over and the Roman Empire as we know it, will be finished! Then, what will they do with you Maxentius?"

Although Maxentius strictly followed the pagan gods of Rome, he didn't want to persecute the Christians. He said nothing as he stared into the crazed eyes of Galerius. He turned around and walked toward the door.

"Don't make me come after you Maxentius!" said Galerius.

Maxentius pretended to not hear Galerius as he exited the palace. He then quickly left and began his journey home.

ADDITIONAL PICTURES:

Galerius' Temple in Thessaloniki, WC, CC

A New Supreme Emperor

Vestal Virgin Statue, WC, CC

Lamb Sacrifice for Galerius, WC, CC

Maxentius, Shakko, CC

CHAPTER 9

BATTLE BELOW

Coin of Galerius CC

Word traveled to The City of Refuge proclaiming that Galerius was now the supreme emperor. Daniel called for an emergency meeting that was attended by over 2000 residents.

He said to the crowd, "I deliver sad news! Horrible news! Galerius rose to the highest level of power and was proclaimed the supreme emperor over the Roman Empire! He will be ruling from Nicaea, just 200 miles away! They have denied Constantine the open emperor position! Get this, Galerius' crazed nephew Daza has been proclaimed an emperor over the regions to the south."

Everyone in the crowd shook their heads in disgust. They were hoping that somehow, Constantine's father would be proclaimed the supreme emperor.

Daniel continued speaking, "Galerius' first order of business was to release a new edict against the Christians. He wants little children to worship him! Imagine that! He has also demanded that they double the number of temples within the Roman Empire! Why? Because when you do not have the Spirit of God, you need impressive buildings, giant statues, and beautiful women to control people! The weak are manipulated by such things!

Should we be concerned? No! Galerius is a false god, and we serve the only true God! Our God is greater! Our God will defeat him!"

The room erupted with applause.

"The weapons of our warfare are not physical but spiritual for pulling down of strongholds! We need to pray this stronghold away! We need to ask God to transform the evil powers that are standing over us!"

Nicolas went forward to the front and led everyone in a passionate time of prayer. Tears were shed and people took turns praying for transformation throughout the Roman Empire.

While Daniel was on his way to his sleeping quarters, he was approached by Stephen and a group of young men.

Stephen said, "Daniel, we must talk to you right now."

Daniel was weary and asked, "What is it? I am tired."

Stephen said, "We would like to go out at night and attack Roman soldiers and put fear into them! They are at war with us, we must be true men and fight back."

"Wait, wait, wait," said Daniel. "Did you attend our meeting just now?"

Stephen lied and said, "Oh yes."

Daniel said, "You are talking about fighting the Roman Empire. Your attacks will only justify their actions against us and encourage them to retaliate! In response, they will send more troops into our region and make our lives more miserable! The last time there were attacks, they sent 25,000 troops into Cappadocia."

Daniel got close to Stephen and asked, "Did Paul the Apostle ever kill anyone? Did not he instruct us to pray and preach the gospel! Better yet, did Jesus ever kill anyone while he walked the earth? Jesus said, 'Those who live by the sword die by the sword!' It is my job to teach you young men to do battle on your knees and lead people to Christ! You will see soldiers come to Jesus rather than death! Tonight, we prayed for the Romans like never before! We need to learn how to share the love of Christ and it will be a matter of time before God breaks through. Randomly killing people and terrorizing Roman soldiers is only going to escalate the problem. Now if you men want to go out and lead people to Christ, that suits me! You can risk your lives sharing the gospel! Isn't that what the Apostle Paul did? Why shouldn't we do the same?"

The men looked perplexed as Daniel left the room in a furious state.

Despite the prayers, conditions began to deteriorate in the City of Refuge. With the expectation of troubled times with Galerius at the helm of the Roman Empire, farmers started hoarding food as prices skyrocketed. The deliveries that brought supplies were almost non-existent to the people living down below. They could not sell their clothing in the marketplace as people held off on purchases. Most of the residents went to bed hungry and everyone was frustrated with the scarce supply of food.

As Christian leaders arrived from all over the world, arguments became more rampant over doctrinal issues. Every discussion turned into a heated verbal battle.

Most people were dissatisfied with their living spaces. Some snored loudly, waking others up. In the middle of the night, arguments would erupt and escalate into disturbing screaming matches.

Oil was becoming increasingly scarce. Daniel kept a stockpile of oil that was strictly used for copying the scriptures. Each person needed oil for their personal space, but when they ran out of their private supply, they would wrongfully take the community oil used for copying.

Eating together had been enjoyable, but in time there was so much resentment, most people would eat by themselves when food was available.

People from various countries stuck to their own kind and stopped interacting. The Cappadocian Christians were becoming resentful of all the foreigners and would complain about them constantly. The wealthy educated Christians would only associate with those that were wealthy, while the poor only associated with the poor.

People started looking down at the escaped slaves that had found shelter in the City of Refuge, forcing them to pound and carry rocks much more than the regular residents. They also received inferior portions of food and were given little or no oil. Their living quarters were also much more cramped, while they only slept in the area for former slaves. They were thankful to be out of bondage, but at the same time, the situation was not fair.

Then there was a huge scandal when a former prostitute was caught sleeping with the person in charge of supplies, trading sex for extra food and oil.

Daniel began to get completely frustrated with the whole experience. When they had started out, there was a real sense of community, and everybody was enjoying living together. Now, he was surrounded by a bunch of angry negative people that were arguing day and night.

Daniel started to wonder why he was working so hard. He began to believe that the end of the world was coming, so what was the point in survival? He sensed that he was living in the tribulation, the last chapter of humankind and soon all would be destroyed.

"Why do I even care?" he would ask himself. "Why even try when we might all be dead soon?"

Discouragement was settling in as deep depression tried to take residence in his heart.

Then one day word arrived that the library in Caesarea had been destroyed. The curator, Phillip, had been tortured and killed. The remaining scriptures had been publicly burned in the center of town. Daniel had to go to the men and women from the library and break the news to them. In the barely lit room, they started crying as Daniel walked away with a deep sense of despair.

That next day Daniel and Ozgur got into a huge argument over the food distribution. Right afterwards, Daniel was walking along with Anasia when they heard commotion coming from the dining area. After running over to investigate, they saw four men fighting on the ground with a cheering crowd of spectators.

Daniel broke up the fight and stood over the four men. One of the men had blood gushing out of his nostrils.

Daniel yelled at everyone, "We are supposed to be Christians! Christians love each other!"

One of the men said, "He stole my bread!"

Daniel hit his breaking point. He asked with a heartbroken tone, "I cannot believe that this is happening. How are we to survive?"

He walked away and met Anasia in their room. Anasia was crying as she vented her pain. "I want out!" she said in her frustration,

"Tell everyone it is time for them to leave. We have done all we can for these people, and I've had it! It's just too much! You would think there would be love here but people have become so selfish and manipulative. We are doing all that we can for the good of others while everybody is fighting! It's a total waste of time! What's the point?"

Daniel had no answer because he was starting to believe the same thing. He prayed about what to do and sensed that it was time to fast. After speaking with Ozgur and Nicolas, the three agreed. The day for celebration of Jesus' resurrection (Easter) was that Sunday. They decided that they would fast for the period that Jesus was in the grave.

They held a mandatory meeting. Nicolas proclaimed, "Daniel, Ozgur and I are sensing that it is time for us to pray and fast. We are at the end of our rope and there will be no work. All of us will only drink water for three days. We will break our fast with communion on resurrection Sunday."

Someone yelled, "How much torture must we endure! We are already starving! Being down here is destroying us! Wouldn't it be better to just die at the hands of the Romans?"

Nicolas said, "We are all feeling the misery of battle. Friends, hang in there. God will deliver us. Let me say it again! Just as God delivered the children of Israel as they stood by the Red Sea, God will deliver us! Please, please, please just choose to cry out to God and have faith!"

People were mad. Some of the residents agreed to the fast but not everyone.

It was a difficult three days. That Sunday, they all broke the fast with communion. It felt good to eat, but the fast felt like it did nothing for Daniel or anyone else. All it seemed to do was make them realize how hungry they were when they didn't eat.

Then something wonderful happened. Later that evening, Daniel was reading the book of John. He came to the part where Jesus prayed for the church (John 17). With a little lamp illumining the page, the words exploded in his mind.

He wondered why he hadn't heard any teaching about the verse before. He realized that the Christian leaders did not teach on this verse because they were not following it.

Daniel met with Anasia and said, "We are outside the will of God! Look at this verse Anasia! We're in darkness! Jesus prayed,

> **'My prayer is not for them alone, but them that believe in me through their message, that all of them may be one.'**
>
> **-John 17:21**

Think about that, our selfishness is getting in the way. He prayed three times in this section that we become one. He asks that we come to complete unity. He's serious!"

At first, she thought he was going mad, but then she realized the weight of the scripture. Suddenly Anasia was encouraged and empowered. Her anxiety and anger left her instantly and her heart was flooded with peace and joy.

"When Jesus prays something three times, he means it!" said Daniel, "Unity is clearly His will. We need to get off our selfish horse and get serious about becoming one!"

Daniel and Anasia were electrified by the topic. Both were excited to proceed with their mission, but with a new direction and emphasis.

Anasia said, "This is the answer! The answer is for us to truly become as one!"

Daniel held her in his arms as he had a revelation. He said to her, "When we were married, we became as one. Our unity has been compromised at different times. We need to share our unity with others! Our relationship is more than just us. God flows through us when we are united! Just look at what he has done with the city."

Daniel met Ozgur and Nicolas. After explaining his revelation on unity, Daniel said, "The division was happening before the persecution. We must change our course and allow God's will to be done. The early church was united, and we need to get back on track. There is no excuse! We're making excuses because we are deceived!"

Nicolas said, "You know, you're right Daniel. We've become complacent. I know that we are outside the will of God and yet, I guess we just don't care. When you stop caring, that is when God will often bring tough circumstances to wake you up. If someone believes the scriptures concerning Christ, then we need to be united with them."

Ozgur asked, "We can't unite with Gnostics and those that are spreading heresy!"

Gnostics were a group that claimed to follow Jesus but didn't believe the scriptures. They put their personal experience above the teachings of Christ. They believed Jesus was a regular man that had a supernatural connection to the spirit world, just like other great spiritual leaders. By putting their personal experience above the word of God, they nullified the scriptures.

Nicholas replied, "There are many that create their own scriptures and those that spread crazy ideas. We must continue to battle them. However, those who uphold the scriptures are all part of our family. We need to be a united family."

Daniel said, "That's right! We must unite. Right now, we care more about our petty little power plays more than we do about the will of God."

Ozgur said, "So what do we do?"

Daniel said, "The will of God is unity. We need to instruct our people about unity and become examples."

Nicolas said, "There are many incredible scriptures about unity. We should pick ten scriptures and memorize them. We will take turns teaching each of these scriptures once a month. By the end of 10 months, everyone will need to know these scriptures. The word of God will transform us and as we pray, we will be united!"

"I like it! Yes, it's a simple plan," said Daniel, "Let's give it a shot."

Nicholas said, "We have the ten commandments, we need the ten commandments for unity!"

They prayed together for unity and chose ten scriptures.

PART TWO

"I have other sheep that are not of this sheep pen. I must bring them also. They will listen to my voice. There will be one flock and one shepherd."

-John 10:16

(Author's note: The underground cities were a secret and discovered in recent history. There is nothing documented about their existence in the files of history. The following segments regarding the teachings about unity are fictional though based on scripture. Nonetheless, Christian leaders emerged from Cappadocia after the persecution, clearly emphasizing the importance of unity. Their teachings transformed Christianity for a season in history.)

CHAPTER 10

MONTH ONE: "BE ONE"

Large Worship Area, CC

Daniel called everyone together for their first special unity meeting with over 2200 people present. Daniel had a sense that this was a defining moment for everyone living down below. Standing up front along with him were Nicolas and Ozgur. Daniel said to the crowd, "Let's begin!"

Just before they started, someone interrupted and yelled out, "When are we getting oil?"

Daniel said, "We just received a delivery and we're going to distribute oil tonight after the meeting."

Daniel paused in frustration at the noise level, but then regained his composure.

"Everyone, I need it completely quiet tonight during the meeting!" blasted Daniel. "Tonight, is an especially important night! Let us start!"

He waited for the chatter to stop. The people could barely see him because the room was dimly lit.

"I was in a far part of the city," said Daniel, "And my lamp went out. I was left completely in the dark. Nobody was around and so I could not see a thing. I stood there, getting more irritated every second. It's just so easy to get irritated down here. But then something wonderful happened. I prayed and asked God to help me. Suddenly, I began to sense the Lord's presence. I just started walking and I found my way. Later I was reading the scriptures and came across this verse from the book of Micah. It says:

>   **'Though I sit in darkness, the Lord will be my light.'**
>
>   **-Micah 7:8**

The Lord is our light down here! We have our lamps, but the Lord is our true light!

I also read in the psalms where King David said:

>   **'Your word is a light to my feet, and a lamp to my path'**
>
>   **-Psalm 119:105**

"If you really want your world to light up, then listen. It is the word of God that truly lights our way not just the oil! We need oil and our lamps, but the word of God is what will truly guide us!"

He continued, "It has been two years since the start of the persecution. God has enabled us to survive this far. I am confident that he will see us through this tribulation. And yet, I'm suffocating down here! Anasia is suffocating! I am sick of the fighting, and I'm finished with the arguments and the division! It is bad enough that the Romans are trying to kill us! We do not need our Christian brothers and sisters at our throats!"

He paused again and then said, "Jesus came to unite us to the Father and to one another! For too long Christians have been divided. We make excuses and justify our disobedience to the will of God, but it is time for us to unite! Perhaps if we are more pleasing to God, he will give us more of his presence and more of his light and freedom. Where the Spirit of the Lord is, there is freedom! If we have the truth, and if God is truly with us, then there is no reason that we cannot get along. Especially down here."

Daniel prayed, "Father, please speak through me and speak to all of us. Let Your kingdom come and let Your will be done!"

He looked out at everyone while Nicolas and Ozgur sat down to listen.

"We had our fast and I must admit that I was miserable, but then afterwards I had the most incredible revelation! I was reading a passage and the words leaped out at me!

"From the book of John (17:21): This is Jesus praying. He said:

> 'I pray also for those who will believe in me through their message, that all of them may be one, Father, just as you are in me and I am in you. May they also be in us so that the world may believe that you have sent me.'
>
> **-John 17:21**

"Think about that! This is Jesus praying, 'That all of them may be one!' Does Jesus pray that we all could have the biggest houses and the nicest clothes? No! But he does pray that we could be one! In this passage he prays three times that we can become one! We all need to get this into our heads! If Jesus prayed three times for unity, then unity is clearly the will of God!

"It would seem in this world, the person who is the most vicious and the most uncaring about human life gains control and power. This is clearly the case with the Romans. As Christians, we have different rules. Christ is different. He rules by example. He is the complete opposite of the Romans! He says that if someone wants to be great, he must become a servant. People will naturally respect the cruel and the heartless person. People respect those who have no conscience and are uncaring about human life. Why do the Romans enslave, torture, and kill innocent people? Because they are selfish and willing to do anything to get what they want! That is why they have power! They are controlled by Satan.

"Hopefully, we are different. Down here, we are seeking to serve and love one another. Nobody is above anyone, and we must all work hard. For too long Christians have been just like the Romans, fighting and jostling for power!

"We must do what we don't want to do down here and that means shoveling feces and cleaning the toilets. That means chiseling and carrying rocks. That means copying the scriptures while torturing our eyes and fingers. It means being a servant!

"Our human nature wants to be Galerius on some level! We want to be exalted as we prove ourselves better than those around us! We want to own the things that bring power and give us control! We don't want to become like Christ! We don't want to become servants.

"Why did the Pharisees want Jesus crucified? Because they were afraid that Jesus was going to take away their power. Why did Pontius Pilate command Jesus to be crucified? Because he was afraid of losing his power! As Christians, we are playing a different game in which we live to please God!'"

Daniel continued, "Jesus prayed:

> **'May they be one as we are one, Father!'**
>
> -John 17:21

Let's think about this, Jesus is praying,

> **Do you believe that Jesus is God? Does God get his way? Does God win?"**

Everybody nodded.

Daniel continued, "You have the Son of God praying that we might be one with one another. God is stronger than our will to come out on top! Right now, we are dependent upon each other for survival! Perhaps he is allowing this persecution so that we have no other choice than to fulfill his prayer! We're stuck in the corner, and we don't have a way out. Let us surrender!"

Everybody applauded.

"Jesus could have come to earth and acted like the Roman emperors, but he came to serve, love, and heal. He came to a lowly nation, to a lowly part of the nation, to a humble woman and was born in a stable. He was not driven by the love of money in his ministry. He rode on a donkey into Jerusalem, called himself a slave and he died a slave's death on the cross!

"John continues with Jesus' prayer:

> 'May they also be in us so that the world may believe that you have sent me'
>
> -John 17:22

"The more that we are in God, the more we are going to be connected to each other and then the world will believe. The world will believe when they see our love and unity. The Romans will believe. God will move through us to reach them as we become one!

"Do you want to get back at the Romans? Do you want to see Rome defeated? Do you want to take revenge? Then unite with your brothers and sisters and watch God move! It's the last thing the devil wants. He knows that he is defeated as we unite and become one. The battle is right here among us! So, if you want to stick it to the Romans where it hurts, love your husband, your wife, your Christian brother! Fall in love with the body of Christ!

To help us to become one, we are going to start praying for unity every day. We have also chosen ten scriptures about unity that we all must memorize. I believe that if we do our part to pray and learn the scriptures, God will do his part and unite us together! The scriptures will become our Ten Commandments. We are going to know them and act on them!

When we are truly walking with God, we can have true fellowship with one another. If we still have our sin, protecting it, petting it, playing with it, and loving it, then we are not going to have true fellowship and unity. We will become lonely, bored, and frustrated."

Daniel called the whole crowd together in a big huddle and said, "Look! God reached the Apostle Paul. Paul was killing Christians, but God stopped him! Yes! Paul became one of the greatest Christians. God can reach the Roman Empire, but we need to do our part and that means unity! Jesus prayed, 'May they be in us that the world may believe!' God can save the Romans. That is how we will win this war! Let's truly unite right now and become one!"

Daniel raised his hands and said, "Will you pray along with Jesus? 'Father, would you make us one, even as you are one with the Father.' Let's all hold each other tight and pray, Father please make us one. Show us our sin and our hatred! Reveal to us the ways in which we are outside of your will. Show us what it is that divides us!"

People started to cry as they let go of their resentments. Others began to repent of their sins. Some people confessed to fraudulent business dealings. One person confessed to stealing oil and repented from being selfish. This went on for an hour. At the end they all sang a hymn to praise God.

Gilley stared at Calista the whole time, oblivious to what was happening. In Gilley's mind, he knew that with women, you didn't get them by being nice, you get them by being a winner. In the room right at this moment, he wasn't winning. He looked at Daniel, Ozgur and Nicolas and his disdain for them grew with each second. They were perceived as winning because they had more control, even though their goal was to bring people into a deeper relationship with God and one another.

He wanted to be in the limelight because in his mind, he would then have power. Power would give him what he wanted. Power would give him Calista.

Before the persecution, he was able to control Pastor Justin with his money. He was also able to control the government with his money. Now he felt weak and worthless and absolutely frustrated. Others were experiencing the presence of God and peace while stripped away of possessions, but Gilley only felt his powerlessness and anger over his loss.

Ozgur got up and asked everyone to pray with him for the Roman Empire.

He started by passionately reading the book of Timothy where it says:

> **'I urge, then, first of all, that petitions, prayers, intercession and thanksgiving be made for all people— for kings and all those in authority, that we may live peaceful and quiet lives in all godliness and holiness. This is good, and pleases God our Savior, who wants all people to be saved and to come to a knowledge of the truth.'**
>
> **-1 Timothy 2:1**

Ozgur orchestrated the prayer time so that people could take turns praying for the officials of the empire, rather than allowing one person to dominate.

After it was over, Gilley walked up to Nicolas and said, "What good is it to pray for the Romans? The Romans are the reason that I'm stuck in this rat hole! We should be using this place to stage attacks. That is the only way to beat them!"

Nicolas looked at Gilley in the eyes and said to him, "Jesus said, 'Pray for those who persecute you. Bless those who hate you'."

Gilley replied with anger, "He will never save the Romans! That's impossible! They will never give up their power! There is absolutely no way they are ever going to change! They understand one thing, power, and strength. We must hit them back with power and strength."

Nicolas stared at Gilley and said, "I believe in the word of God. It says that if we pray, believe, and have faith, God will move the mountains. We will see Romans dropped into the sea and be baptized!"

Gilley replied, "You are so weak! God had the Jews kill all the people when they were invading the Promised Land! Why not kill these vermin? They are clearly our enemies!"

"Because it isn't God's plan," said Nicolas. "God's plan is for us to love them and help them see God in us. Jesus said, 'My Kingdom is not of this world. If my kingdom were of this world my disciples would fight. Jesus also said, 'The Kingdom of God is within you.' Let the Kingdom of God invade your heart Gilley and don't allow any idols to come in. God used the Jews to create an illustration for us. Just as they invaded Israel, God wants to invade our hearts and allow his kingdom to spread within each of us. In the world, the people serve the gods of money, lust, and power. God wants us to be completely free of these things!"

"That's your interpretation of scripture!" said Gilley. "It is all open to interpretation!" He then turned and stormed out of the room, as Nicolas shook his head in frustration.

Daniel went forward and spoke to the crowd. "Everyone," said Daniel, "We are going to distribute oil. Please come forward and form a line. Everybody will receive the same amount."

If the supplies of oil ran out during the time of distribution, the people in the back of the line missed out, therefore people would get aggressive when forming the line. On this night, people were showing much more respect toward one another.

The next morning, there was a noticeable change in everyone's attitude. Residents banded together in groups of three and prayed for unity before their workday. Even though food was in short supply, the people had strength and joy in their hearts.

That night, Daniel called a special meeting, and everyone came together into the worship room. He got up front and announced, "Tonight we have Michael here from New Jerusalem. For those who don't know, New Jerusalem is a city like ours. They have over 8,000 believers all living underground. Just as we are uniting amidst the persecution, we are going to achieve the ultimate feat of unity. We are going to unite the two cities together with a five-mile tunnel!"

Daniel pointed to Michael from the crowd and said, "Michael come and share the plan."

Michael was in his thirties, very tall with a long scruffy beard that he liked to grab and hold while talking. He walked up to the front, looked around at everyone and said, "We estimate that the task will take three years if we are aggressive."

One of the men sitting up front said, "I'm sorry. A five-mile-long tunnel? Have you men gone insane? It's impossible!"

Daniel got up and said, "No, it is possible. My uncle started digging to find water and they said it was impossible. We can do it and we will do it. If we unite the two cities, then if one is attacked, the people can retreat. Supplies can run between the two encampments. Ozgur will talk about how this can happen."

Ozgur got up and said, "In order to unite the two cities, we will have to dig just 12 feet per day. That means we will progress 24 feet per day if both cities dig at the same rate. Then in three years, we should be able to connect the two sides."

Another skeptic asked, "How in the world are two tunnels going to meet? If they miss, the whole effort will be a total waste of time!"

Ozgur replied, "Through several methods, we will be able to coordinate the digs and meet in the middle."

Daniel said, "We've got nothing else to do down here, so let's do what sounds impossible!"

Everyone agreed, even though the venture was a daunting task.

That next morning, they began the tunnel effort. They prayed earnestly as they stood together, arm in arm. Then with unmatched energy and enthusiasm, they attacked the wall to start forging the tunnel as if they were facing an army. In the first two days they were able to extend 50 feet per day, dramatically surpassing their goals.

Meanwhile back in Thessaloniki at Galerisus' new palace, he was feasting on a large chunk of ham. His favorite concubine had just arrived when his top advisor stormed into the room.

He said, "Sir, I bring unfavorable news."

Galerius took a sip of wine with his eyes glued on his concubine. He said, "I'm obviously busy!"

"Would it please his honor if I met with him later?" asked the advisor.

"Oh, what is it?" asked Galerius.

The advisor spoke, "When Maxentius returned to Italy, reports circulated that you were demanding taxation on the citizens of Rome. Rioting spread and in response, Maxentius pulled away from the Roman Empire! He has declared autonomy from you and the other emperors!"

"What!?" asked Galerius.

"It is true sir," said the advisor, "He has also proclaimed freedom for the Christians."

"I knew it!" yelled Galerius, "I should have just killed him when he was here!"

As a Roman Emperor, one needs gifted generals under him in order to conquer. At the same time, a talented general is a natural threat to an emperor. If they demonstrate an elevated level of success, eventually, they will want to rule and become an emperor. Galerius was concerned about a general named Severus who possessed strong leadership skills. Galerius planned to send him into Rome with an inadequate army against Maxentius. After his loss, he planned to go into Rome himself with a superior army and demonstrate his greatness.

When Severus arrived at the palace, Galerius sat him down and explained the situation. He said to him, "You Severus are now an emperor of the great Roman Empire. All the world only dreams of your position and power! You have achieved unfathomable greatness! Now, go to Rome and defeat Maxentius! Conquer Italy and the Western portion of the Roman Empire will be yours."

"Well. thank you, my Lord," said Severus. "Pardon me for saying this, but attacking Rome is no easy venture."

"You must leave now!" demanded Galerius. "The element of surprise will enable you to win! You are talking to a man who knows strategy! Maxentius has never fought a single battle in his life! Surely, he is not prepared!"

It was true, Maxentius was intelligent but not a military commander. Severus agreed to go along with Galerius' plan. However, when he studied the maps of Rome with its walls and high towers, he became overwhelmed with fear.

Nonetheless, Severus was inaugurated as an emperor in Galerius' palace with a quick ceremony attended by only five people. The coveted purple toga was placed on his body. Afterwards he made several public appearances with the toga, men bowed before him in respect and women threw themselves at him. Eventually, the pride of the toga overruled all his sensibilities. Terrified, he made his way to Rome with a small army hoping for the greatest victory in history. Internally, he knew his chances were non-existent.

CHAPTER 11

MONTH TWO: "COMPLETE UNITY"

Underground City, CC

The first lesson on unity was transformational for everyone living down below. The three men decided that Nicolas should teach the second lesson.

Nicolas got up before the crowd and asked, "How important is unity to God? The second unity scripture that we are going to memorize is from the Gospel of John. This is a continuation of the first verse that we are memorizing, and it is remarkably similar. From the book of John, this is Jesus praying:

> 'I have given them the glory that you gave me, that they may be one as we are one. I in them and you in me, so that they may be brought to complete unity. Then the world will know that you sent me and have loved them even as you have loved me.'

-John 17:22

Nicolas said, "Is Jesus calling us to half unity? Is 'ten percent unity' the will of God? Is semi-united, okay?"

He paused and then yelled at the top of his lungs, "He calls us to complete unity! Complete unity! This is Jesus' prayer!

"How is it that we as Christians openly defy the will of God when Jesus says: 'I have given them the glory that you gave me, that they may be one as we are one?'

"We have His words, and we have the presence of God living inside of us! We are perfect in God's eyes! We have the glory of God given to us freely through Christ! I'd rather have the glory of God over my life than what Diocletian and Galerius have!

"With the glory of God over our lives we don't need to prove anything to anyone! We have absolute security! We experience the love of the Father on earth! God loves us with the same love that he has for Jesus! Are you perfect? No, but God still loves you as if you were perfect! You are perfect in God's eyes when you have Jesus!

"Yes, you have something that you do not deserve. God has given His glory to us. You have God's perfect righteousness through Christ and the presence of God in your life! Jesus prays,

> 'That the world may know that you have loved them as you have loved me!'

"Think about that!" said Nicolas boldly, "Not only does God love you with the love He had for His perfect Son, but also, God wants to show the world that He loves you!

Complete Unity

"The Holy Spirit is God's hand that reaches into our lives. We have the Holy Spirit, and we are the temple of God! He lives within each one of us. That is how we can survive down here because God is with us! It does not get any better!

"I've heard that Diocletian has retired at his vacation house on the water with 100,000 square feet of space. He has 5,000 full-time staff serving him. They work around the clock, helping him find happiness. Why would you need 5000 people surrounding you? To create the image and the lie that you are important! However, something is lacking Diocletian! You will die just like everyone else! Your life is a vapor, here today and tomorrow you will vanish away! It's guaranteed! You do not have the love of God in you! Therefore, you are poor and naked! You are worse off than a worm! You are nothing! Knowing the love of God is much better than having 5,000 people around you, longing to grant you your every wish!"

People started applauding and yelling "Amen." Courage and strength flowed into them as they listened to Nicolas.

"You (Diocletian) don't know the love of the family of God. You live in fear because you believe it will all be taken away. You're afraid of everyone, that they want your stuff! Guess what, it will be taken away! All of it! All that you have will never satisfy like the love from the Father through Christ and the Holy Spirit! We have the glory of the living God while he pretends to be a god. We experience the love of the living God while he plays with demons! He fights for power with those surrounding him! Yes, and maybe he has given up because one more ruthless than him has risen to power, but it was bound to happen. There's no way to win at that game!

"I would hate to be Diocletian! I would hate to be Galerius! Do not get me wrong, I would enjoy all their stuff and all that power, but without God, I would be miserable. I would much rather have what we have down here! Yes, we are living like moles, but what does it profit a man to gain the world, and yet lose his soul? The Roman leaders have lost their souls, but we have so much more! Here is a promise from the scriptures:

> 'What, then, shall we say in response to these things? If God is for us, who can be against us? He who did not spare his own Son, but gave him up for us all—how will he not also, along with him, graciously give us all things?'
>
> -Romans 8:30

"We are more than conquerors through him who loved us! We are more than the Romans or anyone who has tried to conquer and kill people to get power. God is with us! He is in us! He is giving us all things! We have his glory! We don't need our own glory like the Romans! We've got the glory of the living God!"

With this word, everyone applauded and stood up as Nicholas continued, "I'm reminded of Joseph. Joseph was sold into slavery in Egypt by his brothers. He could have carried his resentment to the grave over their transgression. Later he was put in prison and shackled in the dungeon. Wait! What did he have? He had nothing in that dungeon while living with the rats and the stench. No! He had the most valuable thing you can have! What was that? He had the word of the Lord living inside of him! God was with him! Joseph spoke the word of God to the Cupbearer as he interpreted his dream. When the Cupbearer was restored to his position and Pharaoh had a dream, the Cupbearer mentioned Joseph. Joseph interpreted Pharaoh's dream and he became a hero! He had to follow God's plan, which included forgiveness and unity. Look at what he said to his brothers when they came to Egypt looking for grain. Mind you, this is after they tried to kill him. This is after they sold him into slavery because of jealousy.

> 'Joseph said to his brothers, 'God sent me ahead of you to rescue you in this amazing way and to make sure that you and your descendants survive. So, it was not really you who sent me here, but God.'
>
> -Genesis 45:7

"He was serving his brothers, the very people that hurt him. I'm sure that while he was in prison, angry thoughts about his brothers came into his mind. However, when he had the opportunity for revenge, he chose to love his family. He chose unity!

"Could he justify throwing his brothers into prison when they were standing before him? How about giving them a little taste of their own medicine? No! He chose to love his family! Today, his life stands as an example for us!

"Guess what! We are all part of the family of God! You can't walk away! If you want the will of God, you will accept your family! If you are in the will of God, you are going to be like Joseph and help those that hurt you. Try helping them by being an example. Therefore, we don't have any excuse to not be united! There are husbands hurt by their wives right here that are struggling. There are wives hurt by their husbands! There are children hurt by their parents and parents that have been abused by their Christian kids!"

He paused as he looked around and continued, "it says:

> 'They will know you are my disciples if you have love for one another.'
>
> -John 13:35

Jesus also said:

'Apart from me you can do nothing.'

-John 15:5

"Apart from Jesus you do not have love. We need his love to fill us so that we can become one. The main way to get in touch with his love is by learning the scriptures. That is why we are praying every morning for unity and memorizing the scriptures.

"I was one of the overseers of a church in Cappadocia for over 12 years. Before the persecution, there was constant fighting between the church leaders. We must ask, 'Were we living as one before the persecution?'

"Greed, according to the Apostle Paul, is idolatry. If you are manipulating money away from your brothers and your sisters, then you are committing idolatry.

"According to the scriptures, the nation of Israel was divided into two countries because of the sin of idolatry. If we stand divided, then perhaps there are idols in the church! An idol is anything we put above God. We were caring more about our buildings than God. Are we more concerned about our positions of power rather than the will of God?

"I saw church leaders speaking against one another. They perceived another church leader as the competition. They would fight with each other for members, fearful of losing their members to another leader.

Remember, when we pray:

'Let your kingdom come, let your will be done.'

-Matthew 6:10

Complete Unity

Certainly, we are praying for unity because unity is God's will!"

Nicolas paused and investigated the crowd and said, "Come on up Jonathan,"

Jonathan was about 22 years old, short, and skinny with a baby face. He was one of the few who would regularly leave and decide what supplies were to be brought in late at night. He would pose as a shepherd boy but bring lambs and other supplies to the City of Refuge.

"Everyone!" said Jonathan with enthusiasm, "We all know that Galerius was proclaimed the supreme emperor over the Roman Empire. But hear this! Galerius demanded that the people of Italy start paying taxes like the rest of the empire. This angered the Italians. Maxentius, emperor over Italy and Spain rebelled against Galerius, even though he is married to Galerius' daughter."

Everyone explosively applauded and cheered.

"Maxentius is stopping the persecution in his area! Galerius proclaimed a general named Severus as the new emperor over the Italian and Spanish province! He is on his way to attack Rome and claim his new domain, even as we speak! Let's pray for God to stop him!" exclaimed Jonathan.

People went up front and started to take turns praying. The front of the sanctuary room was wet with passionate tears.

The next day at the City of Refuge it was Gilley's turn to shovel the feces out of the toilets and transport it outside. To see the stars and smell fresh air, one had to empty the toilets first. Gilley was bent over with a small shovel, placing it into the pot. The foul smell almost caused him to vomit.

"This is ridiculous!" he said under his breath. allowing his anger to grow. He stopped working and yelled out, "Oh my back! My back!"

He told the supervisor. "My back is bad right now. There's no way I can work tonight."

"You can go below," said the supervisor.

He went down into the sick area where Calista was a nurse. He stared at her as he was lying on his back, taking one of the few spaces available for the sick.

Living underground was difficult for everyone. The married couples at least had a companion. It was a different story for a single Christian man or woman. The single people could hear the married lovers at night, and it made them angry.

And then there was Calista. The men would catch glimpses of her and talk about her among themselves. She knew that it was her duty to keep to her work, yet she craved a man. She knew that it was her destiny to someday offer herself to someone. If she were going to remarry, it had to be with someone special. She had to experience the presence of God within the relationship.

Gilley thought that she would be his. He was tall, good-looking, with a commanding personality. All women found him attractive. Calista would glance at him, but she saw past his appearance. She listened to the inner voice. All her life men were approaching her and doing everything possible to break into her world, even after she was married. She was particularly good at keeping men at bay.

The next day, early in the morning during breakfast, Gilley saw Calista talking with Ozgur. Jealousy suddenly inflamed within him. He was losing again, and his mind was torched with thoughts of rage.

Daniel was making his morning rounds to ensure that everybody was where they needed to be. He saw Ozgur and Calista talking. She had a smile on her face and an affectionate look in her eyes. After she walked away, Daniel approached Ozgur.

Daniel said, "So I see you and Calista maybe have a little something going on?"

"What do you mean?" asked Ozgur.

"I mean that you look like you are pursuing her," said Daniel.

Just looking after a poor widow," said Ozgur with a smile as he quoted the scripture:

> **'This is pure and faultless religion, to visit the widows in their distress.'**
>
> -James 1:27

This is my favorite scripture right now!"

"Oh yes," said Daniel laughing, "Caring for a poor little widow. Pure and spotless religion at its best!"

A week later Ozgur and a team of men that included Gilley were working on a new air vent. Gilley was back to work, and it infuriated him to be working under Ozgur. He felt that he should be supervisor and there was a conspiracy.

His resentment exploded, and he could stand it no more. He picked up a large rock and pretended to trip, dropping the rock on Ozgur's foot.

Ozgur screamed in pain as he fell to the ground.

Gilley just stared, saying nothing.

Ozgur tried to get up but could not. He screamed as he attempted to walk on the foot. Others ran to help as they brought a physician over to evaluate him.

The physician said, "It looks like it is broken. You must stay off it or we might be required to amputate."

"Ah!" cried Ozgur, inflamed with pain and anger as his foot began to throb and become increasingly swollen.

When Daniel heard that Gilley had dropped the rock on Ozgur, he was awestruck. Gilley denied that it was intentional, but Daniel knew Gilley all too well. Suddenly all the resentments from Daniel toward Gilley revisited him.

In the dark of the night, Ozgur laid there writhing in pain while thoughts of rage tormented his mind. He imagined himself carrying out acts of revenge against Gilley.

The next day Daniel asked Ozgur the course of action that they should take with Gilley. Ozgur said he didn't want to talk and that he needed to pray about everything.

After a week, they were able to carry Ozgur to the worship area for their services. He saw Gilley during the worship and thought, "How can a man show so much contempt for his brother and yet pretend to worship." To Ozgur, loving his fellow man was one way of expressing his love for God.

To Gilley, it was all a completely different game. Appearing like he was close to God was everything. If he won with money and power and was able to create the image of a godly person, it gave him opportunity to befriend Christians and then get more money and power at an opportune time.

Complete Unity

The scriptures were clear about the importance of integrity. And yet, Gilley had affairs when he was married, lived with a woman he was sleeping with after his divorce, lied constantly in business to get the upper hand. He was an expert at manipulating and controlling people. Christians would think that they were working with someone that was blessed because of all his possessions. Always, he used that image to take advantage of others.

Because Calista worked in the sick-ward, Ozgur was able to spend more time with her. Calista had recently heard the story of Ruth during one of the Bible readings. One evening while everyone was sleeping, she walked quietly into the injury area. She slowly and carefully woke up Ozgur and with a big smile she said, "Hello there. It's me. Don't be afraid."

Ozgur thought he was still sleeping and dreaming, but then he realized that he was awake. She lay down at his feet, putting his injured foot on her stomach.

"What are you doing?" he asked.

She said, "I don't know. This is how it happened in the story we were reading the other day about Ruth. I figured this is how people come together."

Ozgur laughed and said, "Well that works for me," as he remembered the Old Testament story of Ruth. Ruth had entered the area where Boaz was sleeping, Ruth uncovered his feet and put them on her stomach.

"Will you marry me?" he asked.

She said, "Yes, most definitely."

He laid there all night long in awe of God's awesome ways with his foot on her stomach.

The next day, Daniel and Nicolas asked Ozgur about the proper response to Gilley's actions. They were completely surprised when Ozgur said that he was thankful for what happened.

Gilley went to Ozgur and said that he was sorry, Daniel thought that it was obvious that he was pretending. Ozgur accepted the apology and Gilley went on his way.

A couple of days later, Gilley awoke to some real back pain, so much that he could not move.

"Help! I can't move!" he yelled at the top of his lungs for several minutes.

Someone finally responded to his cries, and he was brought to the injury ward. There he saw Calista and Ozgur affectionately talking to one another. Word reached him of their engagement as Gilley was completely confined to a small area. Apart from his agony, he possessed rage against Ozgur. His power was being taken from him and he had no resistance to thoughts of jealousy.

Food supplies were dwindling again. Daniel started receiving complaints about the distribution of food and the man in charge of the responsibility.

Then one day as he was walking into the dining area, one of the men called him over and said, "Do you see this? This is what was given to me!" He then pointed to the man next to him with a much larger amount of lentil stew and said, "This is what was given to this man because he steals oil and gives it to the food distributor."

Daniel saw that the portions were not fair. He privately met with the food distributor and discussed the complaints. The man acted like it was an isolated incident, but others confirmed the unfair distribution. It was Daniel's immediate impulse to want to pull him from the position, but he was learning to prayerfully consider each move. He decided to assign four men to the job, creating two teams of two people each. This way they were all less likely to conspire together. The teams of two were people that were not close friends, but high in character. Daniel personally met with each person and prayed with them, explaining the importance of the job.

Afterwards, there was a dramatic reduction in complaints, and everyone seemed to feel like the system was fair.

A short time later, one of the guards heard noises coming from the entrance of the city. He looked out of the hole in the door and saw some frightening figures that looked like Roman soldiers. He then ran down below, racing up to Daniel. He said frantically, "There are three Roman soldiers at the entrance!"

Daniel called Ozgur and several men together and went up to look through the door. After seeing the soldiers, he said quietly, "We'll smoke them out with sulfur."

Daniel and Ozgur climbed up to the secret lookout vent where they could see the cave entrance of the city. They saw that there were three more soldiers keeping guard.

They went back down below and said, "We've got a group of six. Three right here and three more at the entrance."

"Aren't you worried?" whispered the guard, "They could totally do us in."

Ozgur said, "They don't want to be here. Somebody reported us, but the last thing they want is to be stuck in the desert. So, they will return to their posts and tell their commanders that they didn't see anything."

"Yes," said Daniel confidently, "We need to put our sulfur to good use. With the stench of hell, they will be gone in no time."

"Let's see if that happens," said the guard.

Right then, the men heard a hammer and chisel, as if the soldiers were trying to chisel through the thick round door.

Daniel told the guard, "I want you to climb to the lookout vent and watch them as they run out!" The guard climbed into position and waited.

Daniel whispered to Ozgur, "They're about to get a little surprise."

Daniel crawled up a narrow space above the entrance. He took his batch of sulfur which was tied together in a leaf. Using his lamp, he lit the sulfur packet and dropped it through a hole. Then he plugged up the hole. He then ran down and plugged up the hole in the center of the round door with a rag.

The sulfur fell in an area that wasn't visible to the soldiers, but they could see the light from the burning Sulphur and smell the smoke. Within seconds, the chiseling stopped.

After a brief period, the guard at the vent look-out came back down with enthusiasm.

"Daniel! It was incredible!" said the guard, "As soon as the smoke started, they came running out coughing as if they were going to vomit. Then they looked at each other in dread."

Daniel responded, "Well, that should do the trick! We'll keep the sulfur burning until they leave." Daniel assigned the guard to keep lighting the sulfur packs every ten minutes, making any type of attack impossible.

In Nicaea, a messenger blazed on horseback through the city to Galerius' palace. When he arrived, he was escorted directly to

Galerius. The emperor was sitting in his large, heated bath surrounded by four beautiful female slaves.

"Sir, I have bad news," said the messenger.

"I don't like bad news," said Galerius, "And keep your eyes right here!" Galerius made sure that the man didn't look at the women.

The messenger reported, "Severus came within 60 miles of Rome. Sir, and many of his men... many of his men defected."

"Why did they defect?" asked Galerius.

"I don't know sir," said the messenger looking down, "Severus is dead. The complete army... gone, killed, or defected. I escaped to bring you the news."

"The fool!" Galerius called for his commander. He arrived within just a few minutes, Galerius exclaimed, "Now I will attack Rome myself! I'll need 100,000 of our best and most highly trained men!"

"Yes sir," said the commander.

Additional Pictures

Diocletian's Retirement Palace, WC, CC

Underground City Toilets, CC

Door, Barnard Gagnon, CC

Roman Bath, CC

CHAPTER 12

MONTH THREE: "THERE IS ONE BODY"

3rd Century Christian Art, CC

The next day was the monthly unity meeting. Daniel walked to the front of the crowd as everyone continued talking. He yelled out, "Hey, we're going to get started!"

He was ignored. Agitated, he raised his voice and screamed, "Hey everyone! We've got Roman soldiers at the entrance of the city!"

The audience was immediately silenced.

"We are on lockdown! We will not get supplies so let's get serious about praying! We are in a tight spot. In fact, let us pray right now!"

He asked God to save the soldiers and that they would leave. Then he asked the Lord to speak to everyone through his teaching.

He began his message by saying, "Tonight is our third unity night! I am going to teach from the first book of Corinthians. Paul writes to us:

> 'There is one body. But it has many parts. Even though it has many parts, they make up one body. It is the same with Christ. We were all baptized by one Holy Spirit into one body. It didn't matter whether we were Jews or Greeks, slaves or free people. We were all given the same Spirit to drink.'
>
> -1 Corinthians 12:27

Daniel looked out at everyone and said, "Jesus calls us to be one body! Our ethnic background doesn't matter! Our economic status doesn't matter! You can be a rich landowner, or you can be a poor slave. In Christ, we are all one!

"My hand does not punch my face! My mouth does not bite my hand! It's all one. My hand isn't fighting with my foot for food. Why? Because when my hand feeds my mouth, food reaches my mouth, and the mouth takes the food to my stomach, and then the body brings life giving nutrients to my hands and my feet. It's all one and it's all working together.

"We have many former slaves here and there is nothing that excites me more than when a new slave arrives. I want all the former slaves to stand up!"

Hundreds stood to their feet, but all of them were in groups together.

He looked at them and said, "We are so glad that you all are here. We are honored to have you in our midst. If ever someone does not treat you with respect, I want to know about it!

"People will naturally judge us according to looks, wealth and positions of power. As Christians, we are different! We have to be different!

"I have been informed by some people that our former slaves are being mistreated here. Some are receiving less food; some are receiving less oil, and some are having to perform hard labor all the time. Let me ask you something, did any of the former slaves choose to be slaves? How did you become a slave in the Roman Empire? By finding yourself on the losing side of a war, or you got a huge tax bill, or you were a Christian. Do you know that I was very close to becoming a slave? Nobody chooses to be a slave!

"Jesus said that John the Baptist was the greatest man to ever live. What did John the Baptist have? He ate bugs, wore itchy clothes, and stood in chilly water baptizing people. He died in a dungeon with his head chopped off. Being great is not about your wealth, it is about being in the will of God and being close to God.

"Look at what Jesus did! He washed the disciples' feet. We know that he slept outside on several occasions. He healed people but never charged money. We know he did not have much money available, otherwise when taxes were due, he would have just paid them. Instead, Jesus asked Peter to go fishing and what happened? He found a coin in the fish's mouth. If they were rolling in money, he would have just pulled the coins out of their reserves. They were poor!

"This is from Mark's Gospel about Jesus' example:

> **'Jesus called them together and said 'You know that those who are regarded as rulers of the Gentiles lord it over them, and their high officials exercise authority over them. Not so with you. Instead, whoever wants to become great among you must be your servant, and whoever wants to be first must be slave of all. For even the Son of Man did not come to be served, but to serve, and to give his life as a ransom for many.'**
>
> **-Matthew 20:25**

"Jesus is clearly referring to the Roman government here, the same government that is trying to snuff us out. Christian leadership must be the opposite of their example.

"Who here wants to be a slave? Nobody wants to serve people, but this is Christian leadership people! We are all so off track! We are just like the Romans in many ways! Jesus became a slave for us and died a slave's death!

"You are not a leader because you destroy others. You are a leader because God has chosen you and then you lift those around you. You serve people with the power that God has given you!

"Look at the life of the Apostle Paul. He asked Timothy to bring him his coat while he was imprisoned in Rome. He said, 'Come before winter!' He didn't even have a coat with him! He was serving the people with all he had and paying a dear price. He was sharing the good news about Jesus and paying the price.

"When you are with other Christians at a meeting, don't judge people based on their looks, their clothes, and their apparent wealth. Always look at God's people through Jesus' eyes. He didn't say, 'Go invite the lame, the blind and the weak' so you can judge them.

"Watch out when choosing the leadership of the church. Make sure you aren't choosing with worldly eyes. Paul has some great words for the Corinthians as he talks about the leadership they had chosen for the church:

> 'For you tolerate it if anyone enslaves you, anyone devours you, anyone takes advantage of you, anyone exalts himself, anyone hits you in the face.'

-1 Corinthians 11:20

"If you see Christians acting like this, should you sit back and allow them to take over? The answer is clearly, 'No!

"People too often fight for power in a Christian community in a worldly way. In the end you might have something that looks a little bit like Christianity, but it exists for the leaders. The people in power will come against the good people that are looking for love and unity, forcing them out of a place of leadership.

"Paul would take money from one church and give it to another. The reason he did that was because all the churches were one. Some of the churches were impoverished.

"I have a responsibility to help my siblings not only here, but also all over the world. When you see that we are one, and that believers all over the world are part of your family, then it is easier to give and become less selfish. We are one!

"In this other verse, Paul also includes male and female, saying there is no difference. We are all part of God's family as sons:

> **'For you are all sons of God through faith in Christ Jesus. For as many of you as were baptized into Christ have put on Christ. There is neither Jew nor Greek, there is neither slave nor free, there is neither male nor female; for you are all one in Christ Jesus.'**
>
> **-Galatians 3:28**

"According to this scripture," said Daniel, "People are equal in God's eyes. We have distinct roles as men and women, but in God's eyes, we are all one. Women are no less important than men and must be respected!

"Let us live with that purpose. To see people as one and to help others in the body of Christ!" He paused and then said, "Let's pray!"

After a short prayer, Daniel said, "Jonathan please get up. He is going to give us a quick report on the Roman Empire. He arrived just before the soldiers set up camp outside the city."

Jonathan rushed to the front and said, "Let me tell you something! God is clearly hearing our prayers! Last time I told you that Maxentius had defected. Remember? He is the emperor over Italy and Spain. Galerius sent a general named Severus to attack Rome. When he arrived in Italy, Maxentius sent beautiful women over to Severus' army. They offered the troops gifts if they would defect. Most of them gave in and joined the opposing army. Why? Because everyone is sick of Galerius! Given the choice to risk death in a bloody war for a tyrant, or go hang out in Rome as you eat incredible food and take a warm bath? Without an army, Maxentius captured Severus and killed him.

"The believers in Italy are free! Maxentius is even allowing the Christians of Rome to choose a Bishop! Word is out that Galerius himself is preparing an army to attack Rome. The Christians of Rome are asking all the world to pray. Christians all over the world are uniting to fast and pray for Galerius' defeat. Let's join them! This is our chance to change history forever!"

Everyone cheered with unbridled enthusiasm.

Daniel got up, "Let's keep praying around the clock. No work tomorrow, only prayer and study with fasting. Let the hunger drive you to pray! Nicolas, please come forward and guide us in a united prayer right now!"

Nicolas went to the front with the faint light of a lamp lighting his face. He exclaimed with his hands raised, "God, you see the pain of your people all over the world because of this man. Please do not give him victory. Grant us victory! Save your people!"

"Yes!" screamed the believers with passion.

"Break the power of the enemy that is over us and bring righteous government in Jesus' name! Let your Kingdom come. Let your will be done! Save Galerius, please save him Father! Please stop the spread of evil!"

Everyone screamed at the top of their lungs, "Amen!"

"Wow," said Daniel, "Some powerful angels are coming our way! Right now, we have exciting news about how God is using us. Marcus is here from Thessaloniki in Greece. He has been here at the City of Refuge for about two weeks enjoying our luxurious accommodations."

Daniel laughed and continued, "The Romans destroyed his church, tortured, and killed our brothers and then burned the scriptures at the center of town. Marcus is a silk trader, and he is on his way back from the East. He stopped off here in Cappadocia to bring back a gift to the believers in Thessaloniki. Markus, please come forward."

Markus was in his late 50s with a long gray beard and was wearing a white toga. His voice was loud as he said, "Many of you know that Galerius has a palace in Thessaloniki. Of all the places, it had to be 1,000 feet (about 304.8 m) from my house. His arch is there along with the amazing round temple that he constructed. I'm praying that one day the building will become a church! People think I'm crazy, but God can do anything! Every time I walk by it, I pray for God to do a miracle. Doesn't it say that all things are possible? Why not?

"When the persecution started a few years ago, they rounded up all the church leaders and did what good Romans do. They tortured the innocent and put people to death. Galerius spends a lot of time in Thessaloniki. They think that we Christians are out to kill him because he is trying to kill us.

"They destroyed our copies of the scriptures, but you know what? I have a fresh copy! We are so thankful for the Christians of Cappadocia and the work being done here! Your siblings in Thessaloniki are eternally grateful!"

Markus sat down and Daniel got up again. "Do you hear what God is doing through us?" he said, "We are preserving the scriptures for the next generation! What a blessing to be able to participate in this ministry!"

Daniel paused a moment and then began to smile from ear to ear. He said, "Well, something special is about to happen! Ozgur, stand up!"

Ozgur got up and limped toward the front.

Daniel looked at his good friend in the eyes and said "When I inherited this cave from my uncle, Ozgur had just lost his job with the government because of the persecution. It wasn't because he is a horrible worker. He was fired for not bowing down before an image of the Diocletian. I told Ozgur about the vision that God had given me for the City of Refuge. He responded and we have what we have today, partly because of his faithfulness.

"He's always wanted to start a family, but unfortunately, his wife passed away just after he was married the first time. God brought Calista to us and tonight we are going to marry these two children of God. Calista lost her husband in Philadelphia at the start of the persecution. Calista, please stand!"

Calista stood up from the floor and walked to the front along with Sasa and Val.

"Before we celebrate," said Daniel, "Nicholas is going to pray."

Nicholas came forward and said, "Let's lay hands on them." Several people gathered around them as they prayed for them.

Nicolas finished the prayer by saying, "God would you create a bond in the two of them that will never break! Amen!"

Nicolas then said to the crowd, "I want to share a scripture.

> **'To all who mourn in Israel, he will give a crown for ashes, a joyous blessing instead of mourning, festive praise instead of despair!'**
>
> -Isaiah 61:3

"This is the story of these two wonderful people. Let us not forget the faithfulness of God."

Ozgur said, "I'm just so thankful for all of you. I am also especially thankful for the special person that God has brought into my life!" He looked at his bride and said, "Calista, I only hope that God can use me to bring more joy into your life."

She said with tears, "What can one say? I'm just so thankful for you! I'm thankful for all of you!"

After a short ceremony, the believers began to celebrate their union. They danced and played special music before feasting on a small amount of specially prepared lamb.

As this was happening down below in the city, Roman soldiers throughout the region were called together for the ensuing battle in Rome. The soldiers that were camped out at the entrance of the City of Refuge were ordered to leave their post and join the attack.

After inhaling the smoke from the sulfur, they were overjoyed to receive their orders. Supplies began flowing back into the city, as the scriptures were released into the hands of faithful people for distribution.

Galerius' army of 100,000 men made their way to Rome. His troops were pillaging along the way, demanding food, and supplies from the villagers. All the soldiers in Italy were called in to defend Rome, and so there was little conflict along the way.

It was a slow journey taking three weeks. When Galerius came within 60 miles of Rome, his first commanding officer received a message from one of his spies within Maxentius' army.

The commander reported to Galerius, "Sir, I have just received word that Maxentius' father has come out of retirement. He is now leading the military. Not only are we attempting to take the most fortified city on the planet, but we are also coming against one of the greatest military minds in history! Sir, might I say that we are making a huge mistake!"

"No!" Yelled Galerius. He turned to the officer that was 2nd in command, "Right here and right now, all will see what happens when someone challenges my orders! Take off his head!"

The surrounding soldiers grouped together and pinned down the commander on the ground. One of the men then pulled out the commander's sword. After chopping off his head, they created a sign that said, "Traitor." Then they positioned the sign in front of his decapitated body for the other soldiers to see as they marched along.

Maxentius' father was a former Roman emperor and brilliant military campaigner. Maxentius was intelligent but had never been in battle. With his father involved, Galerius knew that his attempt to seize Rome would be virtually impossible.

There is One Body

Galerius spoke to another advisor and considered the situation. As he saw the walls surrounding Rome, he decided to try to reconcile. He sent a couple of messengers on horseback to go to his son-in-law. He said, "Tell Maxentius that we are family. Tell him that I only want to work things out for his own good. Remind him that he is married to my one and only precious child."

When the messengers met with the officials of Maxentius, they were fed the best food and offered the luxuries of Rome. With Galerius, every negotiation was an opportunity to manipulate. Preying on the opposition's desire for peace was an easy way to get the upper hand. Maxentius knew that he would be foolish to negotiate.

Meanwhile, Maxentius sent beautiful young women to Galerius' camp to meet with the troops. Dressed seductively, two of them approached some soldiers as one woman said, "If you will come over to the Roman side, you will be given homes and freely enjoy luxury upon luxury."

The other girl continued, tranquilizing the men with the smell of her perfume and her smile. She said, "The soldiers that defected from Severus are now living with us in paradise! Why risk your lives for a tyrant? Nobody has ever beaten the forces of Rome so come away and have fun."

The two men looked at each other, nodded in agreement and then ran off. One of Galerius' officers came to him and informed him of the defections.

In the meantime, Maxentius' father had strategically set up his army, knowing beforehand Galerius' likely plan of attack.

After Galerius' messengers returned with word that Maxentius wasn't willing to reconcile, Galerius called his troops together for a meeting before the battle. It was hard for him to fake enthusiasm, but he gave it his best.

The Underground City of Cappadocia

Waiting for total silence, he said, "We've waited for this moment all our lives! Now, we are about to stage an attack on the greatest city in the world! Rome will never be the same. Maxentius sent beautiful women into our camp to try to lead us away. For those who have resisted the seduction, I want to say that you have made the right move! For we will have all the beautiful women of Rome at our fingertips once we penetrate her walls! Get ready to see the head of Maxentius lifted in the air as we parade through the streets of Rome! Let the greatest battle in history begin!"
There was no cheering after his speech, all the men looked down on the ground in discouragement.

The men formed their battle positions and began to move forward. Those up front felt like cattle about to be slaughtered. When they made it over the hill, they approached the walls of a fortress. The opposing soldiers dispersed while thousands of men appeared from the safety of the walled structure. Suddenly a flurry of arrows and exploding bombs began to desecrate Galerius' men.

It was obvious to Galerius that favor was not on his side, especially when he saw more of his troops defecting. A couple of riders broke through the line of defense and charged toward Galerius. He barely escaped as one of the men pulled on his armor. Unsheathing his sword, Galerius defended himself and ran toward the safety of his reserve forces. There were scores of dead soldiers on the ground within the first five minutes, all from Galerius' army.

When the opposition had captured two of Galerius' catapults, his new commander was frustrated and saw that failure was eminent. He looked Galerius in the eyes and just asked, "Sir?"

Galerius looked around and then thought of the embarrassment of losing. He had lost before, and he knew that defeat was unavoidable. He could choose to fight on and die, or he could retreat at this moment and pursue his pleasures.

His commander risked his life by asking, "Sir, what would you like me to do?"

Right at this moment, Galerius thought about pleasure and living only for eating, drinking and sex as he considered death on the battlefield. He said to his commander, "Yes, let's retreat."

The word "retreat!" was echoed throughout the battlefield as Galerius' men quickly turned around and ran. The soldiers quickly regrouped in another area as Galerius addressed them.

With vacant eyes he said loudly, "Make them pay! I want you men to rape and pillage the whole way home! Give them all that they deserve! Make them forever regret what happened today!"

Maxentius' forces began to cheer ecstatically when they saw Galerius leaving. Some men wanted to continue to attack, but they were instructed by Maxentius to permit them to flee.

After traveling some eighty miles outside of Rome, Galerius' team approached a village. He commanded his men to find him a beautiful woman and wine. They attacked a family and captured a 15-year-old girl. They tied her up inside a barn as Galerius went to her.

The embarrassment of losing and the reality of his weakness was unbearable for Galerius. The shame of failure overturned everything within him. There were only three things that he desired at this moment that took away the shame: food, drunkenness, and sex.

Inside the City of Refuge, Gilley was back to his old ways and set up an independent leadership committee. He pretended not to be involved. His group of men called Daniel and demanded that he meet with them. Daniel agreed and called on Nicolas and Ozgur for the meeting.

David, an elder from Daniel's old church, started things off by saying, "There are way too many mistakes being made down here! Obviously, others with wisdom need to participate in the decisions of this city. You three are taking on too much responsibility and making all the wrong moves."

Despite all the sacrifices of Daniel and his friends, these men were interested in one thing: acquiring power. The acts of selflessness were perceived as a sign of weakness to be exploited.

The group had even considered taking over The City of Refuge by force. They discussed stealing the swords and containing Daniel and the two other men. One of them refused for fear of an uprising afterward. He stated that there were too many people that respected the leadership and overthrowing them would not work.

Daniel addressed the men, fully aware of their motives. "Gentlemen, why are you here?"

David said, "To survive."

Daniel said, "Well you are surviving."

Nicolas added, "We respect your wisdom, but we all must seek the Lord. I do not see any of you serving here wholeheartedly. Humble yourselves and God will lift you up. As Christians, you have nothing to gain by being a facilitator of the work of God, except to be more pleasing to the Lord. If you truly want power, join the Roman army, start killing people and fight your way to the top! We're playing a completely different game!"

Daniel interjected, "Clearly, we are not perfect. Now, if you believe that God has called you to leadership down here, just work hard and be more of a servant. Copy more scriptures and pound through more rocks. Start helping people all the time! Die to your evil ambitions and fears! But if you have a problem with the calling that we're fulfilling for your own good, then please do us a favor and just go someplace else!"

David raised his voice, "Will you stop it with your ridiculous rubbish! You are the most manipulative person in the world. Let's face it!"

The Roman method was to use force, deceit, and any means possible to gain power. Daniel's method was to serve and be an example as the Spirit of God led him. David was trying to appear strong. If he could criticize someone else, he could gain power. He knew that people naturally follow the person that appears strongest. By yelling at Daniel, he appeared to be the most powerful person.

One of the men asked Daniel, "What is going to happen to this city once the persecution is over? You will own it, so we are all just working for your benefit! What's to stop you from turning this into a Christian retreat Inn, charging people to stay here? Also, is anyone paying for the scriptures that we are copying? These are questions that we are not afraid to ask."

Daniel knew that he was being tested. His natural inclination in this moment was to raise his voice in response. He looked at the other men and said in a calm manner, "Let me ask you something. If you find out that we are simply serving God, will that change your attitude? Will you men start working on the tunnel, picking up the refuse from the toilets and doing the things must be done for us to survive?"

He waited for a response but did not get one.

Daniel continued, "The City of Refuge is a sacrifice to the Lord. We might need to return here in the future if persecution ever occurs again. Therefore, it will always remain a secret. For your information, we do not make any money on the scriptures we copy and distribute. We do it for the good of the churches all over the world. May God bless us for our efforts. All the money that we receive from contributions goes towards supplies. There's no stockpile of cash. It is all being used."

Daniel then looked around at the men and said, "Enough!"

He walked away infuriated as he went to his quarters. He proceeded to cry out to God for strength and wisdom. Later that night, Daniel, Nicolas and Ozgur had a short meeting. The three men decided that it was time to kick Gilley out for good, believing that he was behind the meeting. They met with him and discovered that their hunches were true. They told him that he was causing division and that he needed to leave at once, but then he began to beg for forgiveness to the point of tears.

They discussed the situation privately. Ozgur read the scripture from the words of Jesus that says, "if your brother asks for forgiveness, forgive him.'

Ozgur paused and then looked at the other men, "How far should we take the teachings of Christ? As much as I absolutely can't stand Gilley, he asked for forgiveness, and we have to forgive him."

Daniel said, "The man is manipulative and will do anything to get his way. He could be asking for forgiveness to entangle us."

"And yet the scriptures are clear. Who here hasn't needed grace?" said Ozgur.

"Is it grace or is it just us being stupid?" asked Daniel.

"I don't know," said Ozgur, "but God can take care of Gilley if we are in the right."

"Your faith always impresses me," said Daniel, "But I don't see how this can ever work."

They met with Gilley and demanded that he change his attitude. When they tested him, he did not know any of the unity scriptures. He promised that he would change and work as a member of the team. The men decided to give him another chance considering the scriptures.

A week later, Hermes and a team of men were excavating rock to create a new sleeping area. As the men pounded away, a big chunk of shiny brilliant metal fell to the ground.

One of the men said, "Oh my gosh!" as he grabbed it and held it up to his lamp.

"It is what I think it is?" asked another worker.

"Don't tell anyone," Said one of the men, "and we'll split the proceeds of the sale when we get out of here."

"No," said Hermes looking his coworker in the eye, "After all these people have done for us and all that God has done to keep us safe, we must turn it over."

He left and returned with Daniel and Ozgur.

When Daniel saw the metal, he exclaimed, "Not only have we found Sulphur, but now we have also found gold down below! Now we can buy more supplies!"

When the man saw Daniel's response, they were convicted of their selfish attitude.

Later Daniel thought about the gold. He considered that the property belonged to him, and that the gold should also remain in his possession. Then he considered the desperate need in the moment, which surpassed his desire for wealth. He reflected on his commitment to sacrifice the property to the Lord, knowing that feeding people and the survival of the community was much more important than his personal wealth.

Then he suddenly got a thought that delighted him in his spirit and that caused fear within him at the same time. He had heard about a Christian that took the gold from the altar of his church and used it to bribe soldiers to release slaves. He struggled with the thought. He then decided, yes, this was God's will. Again, his mind went back to the idea of hoarding some of the gold for himself. He remembered that God delivered him from becoming a slave when he owed a huge tax bill. He decided that he would completely sacrifice the gold over to God, even though it was hard for him to do this.

Additional Picture

Roman Soldiers, Gary Todd, CC

CHAPTER 13

MONTH FOUR: "KEEP THE UNITY OF THE SPIRIT"

Underground City, Nevit Dilmen CC

The next night they began their monthly unity meeting. Nicolas started things off by saying, "Many of you know that we have found gold here in the City of Refuge. It is a huge deposit! Much larger than we originally reported."

Everyone cheered loudly as Nicolas waited for people to quiet down.

"With this gold, we will be able to buy supplies! We found water here, we found sulfur and now we have found gold! There is no doubt that God is taking care of us. If we're smart, we'll have plenty of food and oil with the proceeds. However, Daniel also wants to use the money to bribe soldiers to release Christian slaves and bring them here."

The crowd was silent.

"Daniel, please come up and explain," said Nicolas.

The Underground City of Cappadocia

Daniel walked up front and said, "There is one good thing about dealing with corrupt people. Everything has a price. We will bribe the soldiers that are overseeing the Christian slaves and bring them here! From what I can tell we have more gold than we need to feed everyone here, so let's put our money to good use! If you are doing excavations and you find gold, please contribute it to the community. We are all working together here for the common good," said Daniel.

"Tonight, Nicolas will be speaking. Let's give him our full attention!"

Nicolas walked forward and began his message, "Let's uncover the gold in the scriptures! I want to read Paul's letter to the Ephesians. It says:

> **'Be completely humble and gentle; be patient, bearing with one another in love. Make every effort to keep the unity of the Spirit through the bond of peace. There is one body and one Spirit, just as you were called to one hope when you were called; one Lord, one faith, one baptism; one God and Father of all, who is over all and through all and in all.'**
>
> **-Ephesians 4:10**

Nicolas prayed, "Speak through me Lord, your servant."

He continued 'Be completely humble and gentle.' To be united, we must be humble. What is one of the main causes of division? Pride! Thinking of yourself above others. The scripture calls us to be completely humble and gentle. We are called to be patient and love one another. This is a command from the scriptures!

Jesus said:

Keep The Unity of The Spirit

> **'This is my command, that you love one another just as I have loved you.'**
>
> **-John 15:12**

"Love is the force that binds us together. Without love we are divided. We are commanded to love as Jesus loved us. Who here is fulfilling this command?"

He waited to see if someone would put up their hand.

"Nobody raised their hand! We all fail! This scripture will keep you humble because we are all failing at Christianity! To be a Christian means to be Christ-like and we are all failing! The only reason we are all here is because of grace. We all need grace! We must receive grace and we must give it away. God accepts us because of His grace. Therefore, we need to accept ourselves and one another! There must be grace present to have unity!

"When you are with someone, they ought to feel as though they are spending time with Jesus. He is meek and lowly at heart, willing to work as a carpenter, willing to serve others... all the way to the cross!

"Look at what it says here, 'Make every effort to keep the unity of the Spirit through the bond of peace.' When do you give up on someone? It says, 'Make every effort.' That means you try as much as you can!

"When you forgive someone down here after they said something offensive, or when they steal your sleeping spot, you are being like Jesus. Ask the person to kindly move. If they are unwilling, come to one of us. But don't hold onto resentment! Our resentment repels us from one another. Satan is doing everything he can to break our unity. When you don't forgive, you are creating a foothold for Satan! Think of the word, 'foothold.' It is like the devil has your foot in his mouth.

"If you are married, the devil doesn't want you to stay united with your wife or husband. He does everything he can to break up that relationship. The devil is making every effort to get you to break down the unity of the Spirit. He wants you to look at all the beautiful women around town as he whispers into your mind, "You deserve that, divorce your wife!"

"Right when your husband was rude to you, the devil tells you, 'You married the wrong man, but there is still opportunity to pick someone else. Punish him and divorce him!'

"Why do Christian's divorce? Usually because there is not enough love!" He paused as he looked at the married couples. "When Christians divorce, they do not have marriage problems, they have unity problems! They have love problems!

"When Jesus went to the cross, did he feel like going to the cross? Did he say, hey everybody, can't wait! This is going to be so much fun!

"No! But he endured because of His love for the Father and his love for us. Endure because of your love for God or your love for your kids. Endure for your love for your spouse! Fight for the will of God as much as you can. He fought for you.

"When you read about the Jews during the days that they entered the Promised Land, the scriptures show that they defeated their enemies. Was it because they were stronger? Was it because they had better weapons?

"No! It was because God was with them! That was all they had and that was all they needed to win! The battle is right here among us. The real crux of the battle for us is to maintain unity! This is what pleases the Lord! As we stay united together, God will miraculously bring us victory!

"Let us maintain our marriages. Let us make our relationships with our kids healthy. Let us keep the integrity within our Christian business relationships. Let us keep all our relationships with one another vibrant and alive.

"Let's bear one another. Let's keep the unity of the Spirit through the bond of peace. God has us here to test our love for him! God has you in marriage to test your love for him! That person at their worst is an opportunity to show love. Kids make a mess in their diapers and mothers change them and endure because of love. Love your husbands! Husbands love your wives! When we love each other, we are loving God! 'This is my command, that you love one another... even as I have loved you,' Jesus also says, 'If you love me, you will keep my commands.'

"It's tough, but we must try harder! At times, His love will flow from us, and our cups will run over! If we do not try and simply give up, we will not experience his love flowing through us toward one another. Loving is tough!

"There are moments when we must move away from people as the scriptures proclaim. In marriage, that moment is when someone commits sexual immorality. You can still stick it out in marriage, but according to the scriptures, you are free to move on if you so choose.

"The scriptures teach that in marriage, if someone parts, they must get back together with their spouse if the two are believers. You can't just move on and find someone else. If adultery is committed with another person, then that opens the door for a couple to part.

"Couples need to stay together! Churches need to stay united together!

"It's only going to happen through love as we make 'every effort' to maintain unity. It is only going to happen as the Holy Spirit moves within us. This is the work of God and not man. Amen!"

"Amen!" roared the crowd.

Nicolas then prayed, pleading with the Lord to pour out the true love that leads to genuine unity. Then he invited Jonathan to come to the front and give a report on the Roman Empire.

Jonathan jubilantly jumped to the front and said, "I can hardly contain myself because of what I am about to tell you! Does God answer prayer? Yes! Especially when we fast and especially when we unite!"

He continued, "Do we have weapons? It says:

> **'The weapons of our warfare are not carnal, but spiritual for the pulling down of strongholds!'**
>
> **-2 Corinthians 10:4**

"Our God is pulling down the stronghold known as Emperor Galerius! This evil man attacked Rome to fight his son-In-law Maxentius. He came very close to the city and then after suffering severe losses, he yelled, "Retreat!" Then he told his men to rape and pillage all over Italy on their way home. He is losing popularity all over the empire, except with his troops who have free reign to do more and more evil. Christians throughout the world are celebrating. Hopefully, this will mean the beginning of the end of Galerius! Let's continue to pray!"

They all gathered at the front to pray after hearing the report. Daniel, Ozgur and Nicolas were greatly encouraged by the news.

One of the young men went to his room and brought back something that he was hiding. He walked up to Daniel and said, "I need to give this to you."

Daniel grabbed the object and held it up to the light. It was a huge chunk of gold.

He laughed as he jested, "I've been looking all over for this!"

"Daniel, I'm so sorry," said the young man to the point of tears, "I don't know why I wrongfully took it."

"I know why you did it! It is worth a lot of money and the devil lied to you, and you believed him. It was a test. The good news is that you changed your mind," said Daniel.

"I'm ashamed! We were working on the tunnel, and we saw a vein of gold as we forged through the rock. I just couldn't let it go!"

"I forgive you," said Daniel, "Don't do it again. Let's all be a part of the community together."

From that one chunk of gold, the City of Refuge was able to finance the cost of operations for two full months. They were also able to free a Christian slave. When the slave arrived at the city, Daniel introduced him to the young man that was hoarding the gold. Tears erupted in the young man's eyes as they embraced each other.

Meanwhile, Galerius arrived in Thessaloniki late at night on his way back from his failed attack of Rome. He approached his victory arch in a drunken state on horseback. It was his tradition to stop whenever he entered the city and look at the depictions of his victories, and then travel through the arch. His men watched and wondered what he would do.

He stopped, took a drink from his bottle as he got off his horse. Then he walked up to the arch and looked at all the depictions. Then he took his bottle and broke it on the arch. He then walked around the arch, fully aware that his men were watching. He then slowly walked to his palace a few hundred feet away his horse by his side.

His staff was terrified when they heard the door open and then slam shut. Immediately Galerius yelled at one of his servants, "Get me ham, wine and prepare the bath!" Then he called for his female slaves as he began his new life dedicated purely to pleasure.

In his hallway stood an original twelve-foot marble statue of Alexander the Great. It was a priceless piece that Alexander had made for himself just before he died. He stared at the statue and then ran over to it and kicked it with all his might. The treasure fell to the ground, decapitating the image of Alexander and breaking off the arm.

His servants looked on in disgust and fear.

A few days later, one of Galerius' messengers arrived. The emperor was sleeping mid-day in his huge bed, unshaven and in a drunken state while wearing his purple toga with his hairy stomach exposed. Two of his favorite concubines sat in the corner with two guards watching over them.

When he was awakened, he became outraged and screamed, "Don't bother me peasant! Can't you see I'm sleeping!"

The messenger persisted.

"Then this better be important," yelled Galerius.

"Constantine's father has died," said the messenger. "The troops have chosen Constantine as the new emperor for the northern part of the empire."

"Great! So now we have two rogue emperors!" said Galerius with rage. "So much for Diocletian's ridiculous four emperor system! Get out now!"

The messenger turned and walked away, but then Galerius called the man back into the room. He demanded, "Prepare a letter for Diocletian and deliver it to him at once! Tell him that the Roman Empire is falling apart. Let him know that he must meet with all the emperors right away!"

The messenger left and returned two weeks later. He noticed that Galerius had gained weight in a short time and was still in bed mid-day. Next to him was a tray with half eaten delicacies. He handed him a letter from Diocletian and a head of cabbage. Galerius examined the cabbage and then read the note:

> "**If you could present the cabbage that I planted with my own hands to your emperor, he definitely wouldn't dare suggest that I replace the peace and happiness of this place with the storms of a never-satisfied greed (15).**"

With a smile, Galerius said, "I'm so glad that the man has found true happiness!" He took the cabbage and threw it up against the wall with all his might. He gnashed his teeth and then turned to the messenger and said, "The fool! I have no other choice but to kill him! I want 10,000 troops prepared right away!"

Galerius' advisor heard the commotion and entered the bedroom, calming him down. After gaining his composure, Galerius said to his messenger, "I want you to write down the following to Diocletian, "If the Roman Empire falls apart, I assure you that your piece of paradise will be infiltrated by greedy lawless barbarians!

I could care less about you, but oh, what is to come of your cabbage!"

"Now get out!" yelled Galerius to the messenger.

As Galerius sunk deeper into consuming more alcohol and having more frequent orgies, he became more violent and more easily agitated.

Diocletian was in his garden tending to his radishes when the messenger arrived and handed him the paper. After reading the document, he said, "He makes a good point. Tell him that I will meet at the Danube."

He was referring to a Roman fortress that was close to his residence. Arrangements were made to meet with the other emperors as soon as possible.

Meanwhile, back at the City of Refuge, supplies were in short supply. The city had a winery that was used to make wine for communion and special celebrations. The man overseeing that responsibility was named Arram. He owned his own winery before the persecution. When he came to The City of Refuge, he started overseeing the process of making wine.

Arram suffered from a drinking problem and had become hardened to change. The pain from his loneliness and failures were numbed by alcohol. After he had been assigned to this position, he began to go into the winery at night and drink an excessive amount of wine in the dark, all alone. He was also giving some away to get a greater portion of food and oil.

One day Daniel wondered why there was only a small amount of wine available for communion. He then realized that Arram was not accountable to anyone.

When Daniel confronted him on the amount of wine that was available, Arram said, "Oh, I know. I accidentally spilled most of it. I'm very sorry."

This response obviously didn't sit right with Daniel. Daniel asked Arram to share the responsibility with another brother, but Arram erupted and said, "You don't trust me! How is that supposed to make me feel!"

"I trust you," said Daniel, "but food and drink are in short supply. Everybody has and needs accountability."

"Then I'm leaving!" exploded Arram! The thought of living without alcohol was too much for him. As he made plans to go, he realized that death at the hands of the Romans awaited him. The next day he confessed to Daniel that he had been taking the wine as he promised to change.

Daniel commended him for his honesty but took him out of his position. Two other brothers took over the winery.

Daniel said to Arram, "Arram, we forgive you. There is grace. We must have grace toward you. But do you see how sin disconnects us from each other?"

Arram said, "Yes, it made me want to hide and at the same time, I found myself getting more and more angry towards everyone."

"That is what sin does," said Daniel, "It makes you want to hide from God and his people, just like Adam and Eve after they sinned in the garden. They were hiding from God. The bond of peace in your relationships dissolves away because there is no peace when you are in bondage."

"Life is so hard," said Arram.

"I know," said Daniel, "Life is hard for us down here. I'm proud of you for your honesty. It's hard but our God is greater than our struggles! Let's face it. You were addicted before you came down here. The presence of God will give you the true peace and joy that you were trying to achieve with the wine. The scriptures teach us, "Do not be drunk with wine but be filled with the Holy Spirit. We need the Spirit to fill us and give us unspeakable joy in the Lord!"

Arram got up in front of everyone and publicly asked for forgiveness. He encouraged others to turn away from their secret sins. He also asked everyone to pray for him to be filled with the Holy Spirit.

Daniel made sure that Arram was in one of the unity prayer groups and was memorizing the scriptures. Arram found some people that were also struggling with drinking too much alcohol. He shared with the members in his group that alcohol was something he could never control, and that for the rest of his life, he would never drink. The others made the same commitment. Through the relationships of this group, the peace of God flooded his heart. He became infinitely happier than when he had been dependent on wine.

ADDITIONAL PICTURES:

Arch of Galerius, Shamaramanic, CC

CHAPTER 14

MONTH FIVE: "ONE VOICE"

Large Underground City Meeting Room, CC

A few days later, Ozgur limped up to the front for the monthly unity meeting. He started by saying, "We are enduring a tough time right now and we need encouragement! We'll be reading from the book of Romans, but first let's pray."

They prayed and then read the scripture:

> 'May the God who gives endurance and encouragement give you the same attitude of mind toward each other that Christ Jesus had, so that with one mind and one voice you may glorify the God and Father of our Lord Jesus Christ.' Accept one another, then, just as Christ accepted you, in order to bring praise to God.'
>
> -Romans 15:5

Ozgur said, "I'm reminded of the time that Paul and Silas were in prison for spreading the good news in Philippi. Their bodies were brutally tortured at the hands of the officials of the city and then then they were thrown into jail. They began to worship God during the worst of circumstances. How can you be thankful when your wounds are fresh from the painful lash of the whip? Despite their wounds, they worshipped God by singing praise! What happened? They were supernaturally released from prison! There was an earthquake, and they were free to leave, but they stayed to share the good news with the jailer!

"I believe the same thing will happen to us. As we unite and worship with our whole hearts, we will be supernaturally released! This persecution will stop, and we will see the Romans get saved!"

Ozgur continued, "God gives us the endurance and encouragement that we need to get along with each other. We can't endure this experience without His presence and peace! With God's encouragement, we can forgive each other and let go of our resentments. As we do this, we are fulfilling his calling to be united. As we endure, despite the weaknesses and failings of those around us, despite our hurts and pains, we will succeed and please the Lord!

"Let us accept each other as Christ accepted us! Were you a sinner when he accepted you? Yes! You are still a sinner! If sin is like a stench, you were smelling like a dead disgusting rat, but he still accepted you and you still smell! He is not going to give up on you, why do we give up on one another? Let's follow his example and endure! Let us consider how Christ accepted us, knowing that he can give us the strength we need!"

Daniel and Nicolas went up to the front and hugged Ozgur. Calista proudly watched her husband, smiling from ear to ear.

Daniel said, "Wow! Does God speak through Ozgur?"

They passionately sang a song together as everyone became even more enthusiastic about the future.

Nicolas got up and said, "I'm going to lead us in the bread and the wine for communion."

Everyone sat down.

Nicolas said, "Paul wrote to the Corinthians and said that when they have communion, they must examine themselves. Is there anyone here that needs forgiveness? Is there a sin that we need to confess? Is there someone that we need to forgive?"

Ozgur stared at Gilley. He knew that he needed to forgive him again and with his whole heart. While staring at him, he ate the bread and drank the wine.

Daniel got up and said, "We have encouraging news for everyone. Dorothy, would you come forward and give us a report on the empire? For those who don't know, Dorothy transports the scriptures out of The City of Refuge. Every couple of weeks, she sneaks out of here with the precious cargo."

"Go ahead Dorothy," said Daniel.

The short dark-haired woman in her thirties began by saying, "I just want everyone to know that God is answering our prayers! I recently heard word that Galerius' wife, Valeria, the daughter of Diocletian, has accepted Christ along with Priscilla, Diocletian's wife. The wives of these evil men are believers!

"Constantine's mother, Helena, is also a Christian. Helena shares Jesus with her son constantly! We don't know if he is a Christian or not. Either way, he's a better man than the other emperors. Breakthrough is starting and it is happening through the women. Don't give up! We will not give up until we have total victory and total freedom!"

Daniel got up and said, "Let's praise God for what he has done. This is amazing news!"

They sang another worship song as people prayed for Helena, Valeria, and Priscilla with utmost passion.

Later that night, Daniel was told that some people were not doing their jobs. He noticed that Stephen from Ephesus was in the kitchen, eating and not cleaning the toilets when it was his turn.

"Stephen," he said, "Why are you here in the kitchen when you are supposed to be cleaning the toilets?"

He exploded and said, "Don't attack me little man!"

Daniel replied, "You are supposed to be in the toilet area!"

Stephen yelled, "I've had it! You are always watching me and pestering me!"

Daniel walked away and grabbed Ozgur as a witness. The two went to speak to Stephen in private. Daniel said, "I don't think you understand Stephen. You must do what we are asking you to do. It's not an option. If everybody just does what he or she wants to do down here, nothing will get accomplished the right way. We're working for our survival, and we demand that you do your job."

Ozgur responded, "Nobody wants to clean the toilets. It's the worst job imaginable. Why would you think that you are above other people and have the right to avoid that responsibility?"

"I'm sick of being here!" said Stephen ablaze with juvenile anger.

Daniel boldly said, "Ozgur, Nicolas and I all have to do it."

"It's degrading!" said Stephen, "I didn't come from a poor family like the rest of you."

Ozgur said, "It's degrading to everyone! Nobody has gone as low as Christ. We all need to follow His example and do what we don't want to do."

"I'm sick of you lecturing me!" yelled Stephen, as others looked to see what had sparked the commotion. "All of you are a bunch of lying idiots and I've had it!"

Daniel said, "Well Stephen, I don't want you to leave but you are free to go."

"I'm finished with this place! Get me out of here now!" said Stephen.

Daniel and Ozgur looked at each other and nodded their heads in agreement.

Stephen thought for a few moments and then said, "I want to be compensated for the letter from the Apostle Paul. It belonged to me. How much are you going to give me for it, otherwise I am taking it with me!"

"Are you serious?" said Daniel, "We don't have much money, but we'll give you what we can."

Stephen knew that he could not sell it above ground. The believers were able to drum up about $500 in gold.

The next night, he was blindfolded and led out of the cave to an area that was close to the road. He walked into town and sold his gold. He began to eat food with the money, devouring the meat from a vender. He also bought wine and began to drink with some men that were standing in a public courtyard. After he was intoxicated, he went to a bordello to get a prostitute.

As Stephan was walking through the market area, one of the soldiers randomly pulled him out of the crowd and ordered him to worship the emperor and to sacrifice. He agreed. The soldier took him to the temple and then led him to the shrine which had a marble depiction of Galerius.

The soldier said, "You must bow down now and repeat the words after me."

Stephen began to shake as the soldier said, "Tell the great and mighty emperor of Rome that you renounce the Christ. Say that you will worship the Emperor Galerius and the gods of Rome. We need you to also say, 'I will serve and worship you only'."

He repeated what was demanded of him.

After he left the temple, an emptiness suddenly attacked him that he had never known before. That night he went out, got drunk and paid for another prostitute. When he awoke, he thought about his horrible decision to leave the City of Refuge. After spending most of his money, he decided to go back to Ephesus.

When he arrived in Ephesus, he immediately met with the Roman officials of the city and began to secretly report the Christians. He used the money he received for reporting people to bribe the officials and advance within the system. In a short amount of time, he became the main tax collector for the city of Ephesus.

CHAPTER 15

MONTH SIX: "PRECIOUS OIL"

Meeting Room with Doors, WC, CC

A month had passed, and it was Nicolas' turn to preach on Unity Night.

He prayed for the meeting and then said, "Will everyone pay attention to this? I want to be blessed. Who doesn't want to be blessed? This is an incredible unity scripture! So here we go! This is from the Psalms (133):

> 'How good and pleasant it is when God's people live together in unity. It is like precious oil poured on the head. Running down on the beard. Running down on Aaron's beard. Down on the color of his robe. It is like the dew of Harmon were falling Mount Zion. For there, the Lord bestows His blessing, even life evermore.'
>
> -Psalm 133

"Let's repeat that last verse! 'The Lord bestows his blessing, even life forevermore!'

"When does God pour out blessing?" asked Nicolas, "When there is unity! How do you become blessed? Blessed are the peacemakers. If you're a peacemaker, you are creating unity and you are blessed!

"The devil destroys the unity and brings division. As it says here in the scripture, the anointing of God flows when we are connected to each other. The oil is symbolic of the supernatural presence of God.

"Satan works extra hard as he throws negative thoughts into our heads about each other, hoping that these negative thoughts will stick! Why? Because he knows that if he can destroy the unity, the blessing leaves. When the blessing leaves, that is when things get ugly and the fruit dies!

"When Samuel anointed David, David became empowered by God to be the king of Israel. In the same way, when we are empowered by God, God can do anything through us, right? We manifest his glory! Right after the oil was poured out on David, he killed the lion and the bear. Then he took on Goliath. After that, he was able to avoid Saul's quest to kill him. He eventually conquered Jerusalem and become a great king to the Jews.

"The oil of God will flow down when we are united! How precious is oil! Oil powers our lamps in this dark place. This spiritual oil of the Holy Spirit powers our souls and gives us spiritual light in this dark world.

"When God calls you to ministry, he makes up for your shortcomings and inability. When the Jews entered the Promised Land, they did not have the ability to beat the people of Jericho, but the Lord fought for them. All they did was march around the city seven times and blow their horns. God made up for what was lacking in their military abilities. Could they brag about their accomplishment! Heck no! Why? Because it was all God!

"The three men that comprise the decision-making team of The City of Refuge: Daniel, Ozgur and me, are doing something that is much too difficult for us! God makes up for our weakness and inadequacies. You do not need to criticize us, because clearly, the job is way too big! Fortunately for all of us, the Lord is making up for what is lacking within us.

"I meet every day with Daniel and Ozgur. Just like everyone, we are memorizing these unity verses and praying for unity. We realize that this is vital for our survival.

"And God is empowering us! I love the last verse that says that God brings life forevermore! Where there is unity, people are going to get saved! We will see the blessing of people coming to Christ! We will rejoice with the angels as we see the fruit of our bond! Just as there are children when a man and a woman is united in marriage, there will be spiritual children coming from the people that are united in heart with each other!

"Jesus said, 'They will know you are my disciples by how you love one another.' What an awesome verse! The world is selfishly ripping itself apart, but when the world sees our love, people will know that we are Christians.

> **'By this will all men know that you are my disciples, by how you love one another.'**
>
> -John 13:35

They will know us by our love, and they will get saved!"

Nicolas turned to Jonathan and said, "Jonathan, come forward and let us know what is happening with the Roman Empire."

Jonathan got up and said, "Well everyone, since there has been division in the Roman Empire, the economy has truly suffered.

Word is out that taxes are down in our region, and this is angering Galerius. The soldiers are angry because there is no money to pay them. So, what is Galerius' solution? The soldiers have been told by Galerius that they can do whatever they want to the public to make up for their loss of pay. They are becoming even more treacherous and ruthless to everyone. On the plus side, because the economy is so bad, Galerius is becoming less and less popular even among the pagans.

"Keep praying people! Times are hard but we are going to get through this. God can do anything!"

Nicholas got up and said, "Amen!" He then turned to the crowd and said, "We have a very special guest with us tonight!"

He paused and then made eye contact with the guest in the low light. "As you know, Daniel and Ozgur showed up at my door three years ago, sharing the vision for The City of Refuge. They wanted to create a haven for believers. I prayed with them and had a sense of God's hand over their work. I knew Daniel was a man of Godly character. He asked me if I knew anyone with resources to help fund the operation. A good friend of mine named Andrew answered. He provides a good portion of the finances for food and oil so we can eat and see. Andrew, please come forward."

Andrew, a skinny short bald man in his fifties went to the front and stood alongside Nicolas.

Nicolas said, "He did not want the attention but I want everyone to meet him so we can pray for him. He is talented in business, and he uses his personal money, while also gathering money from others, so we can do what we do here. Even though we have found gold here, we still need him. We need everything we can get!"

Andrew said, "I just want to say that it is a complete honor to be here with everyone tonight. You people are the true champions for the cause! This is a dark time in history, but God will come through for us," He paused and then said, "I truly need you to pray for me as I travel raising and selling horses. Fortunately, I have never been asked to worship the Emperor and I would like to keep it that way! That is why I need God's help and so I am asking you to pray! Thank you!"

Nicolas responded, "He is an incredibly humble man. He raises the best horses in the world. Diocletian, Maxentius, and Constantine all ride his horses. His horses have won three championships this year! He could be living just for the money and pleasure, but he practically gives it all away so that we can keep this operation afloat."

The crowd cheered.

"Andrew! Thank you!" said Nicolas.

The next day several men were eating in the dining area. A former slave sat at the table with his face branded with the word 'fugitive' on his forehead. He received little food with a full day of work ahead of him. He requested a second portion but the person distributing the food refused him because of the short supply.

One of the other men overheard his request. He said, "Friend, please take my portion. I will be copying scriptures today and clearly; I do not need as much food as you."

"Thank you so much," said the former slave. "I can't tell you how thankful I am!"

These types of events were becoming increasingly common. There was more unity and acts of kindness, but unfortunately, there was another relentless force at work in the City of Refuge.

Gilley and another man were talking during lunch. Gilley said to the man, "Daniel was a nobody a few years ago. He has done a good job of using this persecution to his own advantage. He didn't even purchase this property himself. It was something he inherited because he came from a wealthy family. Me, I am a 100% self-made."

The other man nodded his head, impressed with Gilley.

"I'm just really frustrated," said Gilley, "because I owned several inns. Nothing was given to me, I made it all happen by myself. I know how to manage people, and it just seems to me that things down here must be run better. We are needlessly suffering in so many ways. If someone else was in charge, we would have more food. Everything could be working a lot better."

The man said, "Yes, I agree!"

"Have you heard of the Mountain Inn?" asked Gilley.

"Oh of course," said the man.

"Yeah, well that was one of my properties. You only learn to build a business and gain success by doing things the right way. When this persecution thing is over, I'd like to hire you as a manager." said Gilley, "I can spot talent."

Making promises was his way of gaining favor from people. Most of the workers at the Mountain Inn were underpaid and angry. Gilley would make commitments to raise wages, but then delay the increases before firing people.

Gilley moved from person to person within The City, gaining influence and breaking his commitment not to be divisive.

Galerius organized the meeting with the other emperors at the main Roman fortress in Austria. Diocletian, Constantine, Daza and Maximian (the father of Maxentius in Rome) had all arrived on time, but Galerius was late. They sat in the meeting room on the second floor as they watched Galerius' carriage finally arrive. When he stepped out with his two concubines, they all gasped.

"Oh my!" exclaimed Diocletian, "Somebody likes to eat!"

Maximian said mockingly, "Can we please switch this meeting to the first level? Honestly, I am worried about the floor caving in!"

The others laughed.

When Daza saw his uncle looking weak and overweight, he inwardly rejoiced. He had secretly joined forces with Maxentius of Rome and the two were planning on taking over the empire.

Eventually, Galerius made it into the room. He stared at Maximiam and then turned to Diocletian and said, "We need to start this right now."

"Glad you could make the meeting that you personally organized Galerius," said Diocletian, "Now, let's get down to business." He looked at Maximian and said, "Maximian, your son has broken away from the empire and is now creating his own empire. Everyone tells me that you are helping him!"

Maximian nodded his head in agreement and said, "That is correct."

"There is nothing gained if the empire falls apart," exclaimed Diocletian. "What is your goal?"

He said, "I want to help my son, but also let's face it, nobody likes what's happening to the empire. The empire is crumbling!"

Diocletian raised his intensity level, "Maximian! You have got everything a man could ever want! You have already proven yourself on the battlefield. What is your problem?"

Maximian replied as he looked at Galerius, "How can I just sit back and let this fool bring destruction to us all! Crime is rampant and everyone is frustrated and angry. Meanwhile, this beast blames everything on the Christians while he sits in his palace, getting fat and drunk!"

"The Christians are the enemies of Rome!" yelled Galerius, "That is a fact that has been long established. I heard that the Christians influenced your son and that they are the real reason he pulled away!"

"Let's not turn this into another argument over the Christians," said Diocletian.

Suddenly, at this moment, Galerius was completely done trying. Even though he was being insulted, he only thought of ending the meeting and getting back to his alcohol, food, and concubines. He realized that planning the meeting was a grave mistake. He looked around him and pulled a bottle out of his coat and then took a quick drink of his wine.

Daza interrupted and said, "I don't believe that Galerius should be the supreme emperor."

Galerius looked at his nephew and said, "What a disgusting serpent in the grass! You would be nothing if it wasn't for me!"

Diocletian turned to Galerius and said, "Nobody, not even your nephew wants to sit under you, Galerius. Look at you! Let's make everyone equal!"

The others agreed.

Diocletian said to Galerius, "Are you willing to look at everyone as an equal?"

"Yes," said Galerius. At this point, he was done.

"Okay," said Diocletian, wanting to circumvent conflict and end the meeting.

Diocletian then looked at the other men and said, "Okay, there needs to be cohesion at this point. Constantine, we need to know your plans. Will you promise to stay united with the empire?"

Constantine looked at the other men and said, "Yes, under certain conditions. I agree that we should all be equal, but we should run our areas the way we want them run."

"I agree," said Diocletian and then he turned to Maximian and said, "Will you work on bringing your son back into the empire?"

"The boy has a mind of his own," said Maximian, "I don't control him! Let's see what he wants to do."

On hearing this," Galerius rolled his eyes. He wanted to release his anger but instead, he stuffed his compulsion to lash out. Above all else, he dreaded the thought that the meeting might be extended any longer. He just wanted it to end so he could get back to his pleasures.

After they parted and returned to their regions, Daza sent a letter to Maxentius, giving him an update. The two waited for an opportune moment to make their move to attack Constantine and Galerius.

CHAPTER 16

MONTH SEVEN: "AGREE WITH ONE ANOTHER"

Underground City, Nevit, CC

A few weeks later it was unity night at The City of Refuge. Daniel started by saying, "We are gaining victory! Jonathan has just entered the city with exciting news! I'm tempted to have him share before we get started, but first, let's study the word of God!

Daniel prayed for the meeting and then began, "We've all heard the story of Joseph! He could hear from God and interpret dreams. He had plenty of reasons to be discouraged when he was sent into slavery into Egypt and then wrongly thrown into prison. He could hear from God and was able to interpret the Cupbearer's dream. The Cupbearer was released from prison and later worked for Pharaoh. One day when Pharaoh became disturbed about a dream, the Cupbearer mentioned Joseph to him. Joseph interpreted Pharaoh's dream and was released from prison! It was the living word of God that released Joseph from prison, and it will be the word of God that gives us freedom from our prison down here! Victory is on the way for us as we turn to the word of God!

"This scripture was written by Paul to the Corinthians. The Church in Corinth was becoming increasingly more divided. Right at the very beginning of Paul's letter, he makes a very important statement about unity.

"Let me just say, that we Christians are good at ignoring scriptures about unity. The reason? Because we don't really want God to be in charge!

"The first book of Corinthians (1:10) says:

> **'I appeal to you, brothers, in the name of our Lord Jesus Christ, that all of you agree with one another so that there may be no divisions among you and that you may be perfectly united in mind and thought.'**
>
> **-Corinthians 1:10**

"Please memorize this scripture!" said Daniel, "If you memorize these words, they will become a part of your soul! When you feel compelled to break away from people, remember this verse! When you are fighting with your selfish ambitions that undermine unity, please, just remember this verse!

"Could Paul be more explicit about God's desire for us by saying, 'In the name of Jesus Christ.' Look at the goal...to be perfectly united in mind and thought.

"Perfectly united in mind and thought with NO division! Clearly, we as Christians tend to lie to ourselves as we justify our division! We are in darkness! We ignore the teachings of Jesus and the scriptures!

"Those who believe that Jesus is the only Son of God need to be united! Completely united! Those who change or add to the scriptures are cursed as the scripture says. But those who believe the good news about Jesus Christ are called to be one.

"The book of Acts says:

> **'When the day of Pentecost had fully come, they were all in one accord in one place.'**
>
> **-Acts 2:1**

"What happened after this? God poured out the Holy Spirit upon the united church that was in one accord. These people were filled with joy and supernatural power, but before that happened, the scripture says that they were united!

"Right after the empowering, a lame beggar made an appeal to Peter for money at the temple gate. Peter replied, 'Gold and silver I do not have, but what I do have I give to you. In the name of Jesus Christ, get up and walk.' The man got up and was healed.

"From this moment, the Christians became extremely effective in reaching the world around them. There was resistance, but they were successful. We can follow the same formula today and unite as one, praying in unity. This is really the answer to our problems!

"The scriptures state that Peter was in Ephesus. He became divisive and only wanted to eat with the Jewish Christians. Paul became outraged and publicly rebuked Peter! Paul saw that Peter was fueling disunity and Paul gave him the hammer! It wasn't what Peter said, it was simply what he was doing. The other Jewish Christians living in Antioch started following his bad example and the division was reinforced. Peter's divisive attitude was considered 'heresy' to Paul.

"People will conjugate with the people that are just like them, but we are called to be different. We have a calling to become 'one.' That was Jesus' prayer. 'Father, may they be one.' We are called to be different from the world! The world does this: rich with rich, the pretty people join with other pretty people, same nationality will conjugate with the people of the same nationality. As Christians, we are different! Our calling transcends everything!

"We have a simple mission down here. What is our mission? To spread the Word of God. As we unite and are in one accord, God will pour out his Spirit and bring joy and supernatural power! Without this power, we can't spread the word of God.

"Let's be in one accord with no division. Let's read this verse again,

> **'I appeal to you, brothers, in the name of our Lord Jesus Christ, that all of you agree with one another so that there may be no divisions among you and that you may be perfectly united in mind and thought.'**

This is a command from God! Let's follow it! Repeat after me! Perfectly united!"

Several of the people quietly echoed, "Perfectly united," in a dispassionate tone.

Daniel yelled, "Repeat it again, I want to hear 'perfectly united' loud and clear!"

"Perfectly united!" exclaimed the crowd.

"That'll work for now!" exclaimed Daniel. He then pointed to Jonathan and told him to come forward and give a report on the Romans.

After rushing to the front, Jonathan said, "You know what is amazing. Since we started uniting, the Roman Empire has been disunited and is falling apart!

"The emperors met together, except for Maxentius, the emperor of Italy and Spain, but the meeting was attended by his father. They decided that there wouldn't be a Supreme Leader and that Galerius is an equal!"

Everyone broke out cheering.

Jonathan continued, "Constantine allows freedom in his region. There is absolutely no persecution where he reigns! The believers are flourishing!

The cheering resumed and then silence.

"Galerius isn't stopping the persecution in our area, but it is just a matter of time. The good news is that God is answering our prayers! Look how far we have come! Let's keep praying and keep believing!"

Everyone rushed forward to pray for a complete breakthrough. Holding hands, they were completely united in their passionate appeal.

A few days later, several people started work on a new sleeping area for one of the families. Everybody wanted to be close to the area near to the stairway that led to the toilets. Otherwise, people had to walk a long distance in the dark when needing to relieve themselves.

As they started the work, another man walked up and said, "Excuse me but this area was promised to me. My wife and I have a baby that cries all night long. She keeps everyone awake. We need a private spot."

"This area was also promised to us," said the other man with an aggressive tone, "We're in the same situation."

The conversation turned into an argument. Ozgur heard the two men fussing as he walked by and stopped to listen.

"Gentlemen," said Ozgur, as he grabbed the men's attention, "Let's work this out. Remember the goal here is unity. We all win when we stay united together. You don't win if you get your way but forsake unity. God will bring a wonderful blessing over your life if you are a peacemaker."

Smiling, he turned to the man that started the new work on the area and said, "Are you willing to give this area up for the sake of unity?"

The man responded with emotion, "My wife will be angry because she wanted to be here. It is close to her sister. They wanted to work together and share the responsibility of the children."

Ozgur said, "Fair enough." He turned to the other man and said, "Are you willing to give up your spot in order to maintain unity?"

He said, "Yes. I too have an infant. But I want to be in God's will. It hurts and I feel like I'm letting my wife down, but we'll do what we need to do for the common good."

Ozgur said, "Do you realize, the pain you are feeling right now requires faith. Your relationship with the Lord is costing you something and it hurts."

"I couldn't agree more!" said the man, "It feels like I'm giving up my manhood."

Ozgur said, "No! You're not giving up your manhood, you are becoming a man of God! Come with me. It doesn't always work out this good!"

He took him to a large apartment area that had separate sleeping quarters. It was one of the largest private units in the entire city.

Ozgur said, "Hermes had been with us since the beginning and worked on this area for several years. Well, he and his family are on their way to France with some scriptures. They are relocating so you and your family can have this entire area."

"Oh my," said the man, "This is too good to be true!"

He exploded with joy. When he called his wife over, she started crying with gratitude as she entered the apartment.

CHAPTER 17

MONTH EIGHT: 'BE OF ONE MIND'

Underground City, Musik, CC

The next month Nicolas taught Paul's second letter to the Corinthians. He prayed and then began his message by asking, "Did you know that God's presence in your life is dependent on your relationships? According to the scripture that I'm about to read to you, God will be with you, only when you value the relationships that God has put into your life.

He continued, "Let's read a verse from the second letter to the Corinthians:

> **'Be of one mind, live in peace; and the God of love and peace shall be with you.'**
>
> **-2 Corinthians 3:11**

"You mean that the presence of God in my life is conditional? Yes! Let's let this sink in!

"Be of one mind!"

"What does that mean? Be thinking the same way. Work it out! Be like a healthy family. A family that lives in peace and works out their problems. Work it out no matter what! Why? Because then the God of love and peace shall be with you! Otherwise, you are playing games! If you aren't in unity, the God of love and peace will not be with you! Do you get it?

"It's like when you get around someone that has not had a bath. You do not want to get too close to them! Your attitude when you hold onto resentments makes you smell bad to God!

"Many Christians just do not get it! They think they can abuse their siblings. They play the same manipulative power games that the world is playing.

"You can pretend to be a Christian. But you will be like Saul from the book of Samuel. Saul was living without the God of love and peace. David reached out to Saul and tried to bring unity, but Saul always refused.

"If you don't live in peace with your brothers and sisters, the Spirit will leave you and you will find yourself attacking the good people around you just like Saul! This is the devil's trick! You become miserable because the God of peace is not with you. Then the devil lies to you! He tells you that your fellow Christians are the source of your problems, but it is your unforgiving heart! You will be in pain and then sin will be right there deceiving you.

"Saul was anointed by God to be king, but because he was disobedient, the kingdom was stripped away from him. God then chose David. Saul made David his enemy and he thought that if he could kill him, that his problems would be over. The problem was not with David, it was with Saul.

"It is not by manipulation and pulling people down that you gain power! It is the love of God and his peace that gives you the true power. God sees you performing humble acts of service to bring provision to His community. He then exalts you! Along the way, everyone experiences success! Don't be jealous of the humble people that are doing what God has called them to do!

"Be like David and care for the sheep that God has given you. Do a great job with the sheep, just like David before he fought Goliath. He cared for the sheep entrusted to him, so much so, that he risked his life for them. He protected them from the bear and the lion. What a great shepherd! He risked his life for these animals and then God gave him a promotion. Be a splendid example to all men. That is how you become a shepherd of God's sheep. Lead by example.

> **'Be of one mind, live in peace; and the God of love and peace shall be with you.'**
>
> **-2 Corinthians 3:11**

"Let me say this, if you hold onto your differences and aren't willing to meet at some level, and you are willing to cut off the relationship and shut the door, the God of love and peace shall not be with you!

"Saul allowed his resentments and fears to take control and direct his behavior. There were moments when David could have killed Saul, but he refused. Afterward was Saul thankful? No! He was back on the path of trying to kill David!

"We are all in the same army and we must work together! We need to die to the voice of Saul in our heads that wants to fight the David's around us. We need to live in peace with one another! Why? Because then the God of love and peace will be with us!

"Do you want God to be with you?" asked Nicolas, "I do!"

Suddenly out of nowhere, a young man began to yell from the audience.

"I want what you have!" he screamed, "I want the love that you people have...I must have it!"

Everyone was surprised. Several people gathered around him as Nicolas walked up and looked him in the eye. He asked, "What is your name?"

"I am Dionysis," said the man, "They were about to brand my face. I am a Roman slave and was promised freedom if I could locate you. The Romans are looking for you. I was trained about your ways and learned some Christian gibberish, which is how I was able to get in. I was brought here with a blindfold, but I was planning to escape to bring the Roman soldiers back."

"Well young man," said Nicolas, "God is about to truly set you free from slavery! Whom the Son sets free is free indeed!"

Nicolas took him aside and prayed with him. They set up the water and baptized him that night.

Several men reached out to him and began guiding him through the scriptures.

CHAPTER 18

MONTH NINE "LIVE IN PEACE WITH ONE ANOTHER"

Underground City, WC, CC

It was an incredible month for everyone living down below in the City of Refuge. The teachings were transformational, and everyone's life was benefited. It was Daniel's turn to teach, and he was excited.

"Get ready for this scripture people!" said Daniel as he began the meeting. "This is from the book of Matthew:

> **'Therefore, if you are offering your gift at the altar and remember that your brother or sister has something against you, leave your gift there in front of the altar. First go and be reconciled to them; then come and offer your gift.'**
>
> **-Matthew 5:23**

"In other words, if you think that somebody has something against you, go work it out. Don't come to church until you have worked it out! God doesn't want your money! It's more important to be unified then to give God your money and support the cause of the kingdom! A lot of church leaders won't teach on this passage!

"Remember the story about Cain and Abel? Abel offered a sacrifice that was acceptable; then Cain offered a gift that was unacceptable. God doesn't want your money if you are causing disunity! Your gift will be unacceptable! This is how serious God is about unity!"

There was a long pause of silence as the weight of the scripture hit everyone.

"God doesn't want your worship if you are creating division! He doesn't want you in his house! He is saying, 'Get out! Get things right first, then you can come back!'

"Jesus said:

> **'When the salt loses its saltiness, it is trodden over by men. Have salt in yourselves and live at peace with one another.'**
>
> -Mark 9:50

"He is commanding us to be at peace! We better live at peace with each other, otherwise things fall apart. Do you know that there is a curse for Christians if they abandon God's passion for oneness? Things get bad when the salt of the earth is no longer salty. When we lose our saltiness, what happens? Things fall apart. At times I have been divided from my wife. Anasia put up with me because she is the most patient person in the world. I was going to church, but I harbored anger in my heart toward her. I was causing division and my world was falling apart.

When I repented and then we truly came together, that is when God's presence and peace came into our relationship and blessing started flowing into our lives. That is when God brought all of you into our lives. You know that we never had children, but now we have all of you here and we are so blessed.

"Nicolas often talks about all the division that existed among Christians before the persecution started. Were we memorizing unity scriptures and taking care of business with one another? Were we loving each other? According to Nicolas, we were not.

"The Bible says in the book of Titus:

> **'Warn a divisive person once, warn them a second time and then after that have nothing to do with them.'**
>
> **-Titus 3:10**

Everybody nodded their heads in agreement. Many people walked up to others and apologized. Some people were weeping before the Lord for the way that they had caused division. People also came forward to pray for unity and reconciliation.

Gilley sat in the back of the room reading a book. It was a book that he secretly brought into The City of Refuge, because Daniel and the others would have refused it. It was a popular erotic novel about a Roman vestal virgin that was sleeping with a priest.

After the meeting broke up, Gilley began to experience pain in his chest and his arm. As he walked to his quarters, he thought about his enemies: Daniel, Nicolas and Ozgur and all that they had done to make his life so miserable. He was angry with everything and everybody. He considered leaving and moving to France or Italy or Rome.

The next day, one of his coworkers went to go wake him.

"Gilley," the man said, "Gilley get up!" His body wouldn't move.

The man found Daniel and rushed him to Gilley's quarters. . Daniel put his hand over his mouth to feel for breath. He said, "He's dead."

There was a part of Daniel that wanted to rejoice but he silenced that inner voice. Daniel said, "We will give him a proper ceremony."

They placed his body into a special chamber in the City of Refuge for the people that had died while living below. Nicolas led the funeral service. Both Daniel and Ozgur attended and encouraged others to participate.

Daniel felt like it was his mission to completely void himself of resentment. He saw how God had used Gilley in his life to make him a better person and lead him to The City of Refuge.

One of the men was going through Gilley's belongings and found a huge sack of gold. For a second, the man was tempted to take it away and hide it in his chamber. Then he thought about Gilley and what happened to him. The man brought the gold to Daniel, who poured out the contents of the sack on the table. He laughed, shaking his head. He then turned to the young man and said, "Let this be a lesson for all of us. How much better would it have been to invest this gold in the community? God is clearly testing us. When we are released, we will use the gold for a huge celebration! We'll buy lamb and have the biggest party ever!"

A few days later, two single brothers were working on a new sleeping area for a couple of unmarried sisters that had recently arrived. After getting approval from Ozgur, they started to pound away to create an entrance for the new little apartment. The two men were working hard together. The two sisters were impressed with their ability to make quick progress.

The older brother started criticizing the younger, not because the other man was doing anything wrong. He was trying to make a dominant impression in front of the women, acting like he was the leader by putting down his brother.

The younger brother felt like he was being attacked needlessly. He prayed that he could be united with his brother, hoping to fulfill Jesus' prayer.

He took his older brother aside and said, "I am trying to show love, but I sense that you are putting me down for no reason. We both are working hard and have a mutual goal to be a blessing to the new women. Why can't we just have that focus?"

"You're being ridiculous!" yelled the older brother, but then he took a moment to think about how he had been treating his brother. He also considered the unity scriptures and the teaching from the night before. He was convicted and began to watch his words, acknowledging that he was in fact creating division.

The two brothers worked hard together and completed a great space for the women. Their hopes were realized and each one of the brothers was able to marry one of the sisters.

It was an amazing month for the people living underground. They were developing a harmony in their relationships that made up for the challenges of living below.

Back at Galerius' palace, his top four advisors saw the horrible impact that the persecution was having on the state of the empire. With record crime and the horrible economy, they decided that they would cast lots to see which one would talk to Galerius. The loser walked into Galerius' room while he was gorging on a big slab of beef in bed, using only his fingers. The advisor reported, "Sir, even though we continue to torture, enslave, and kill the

Christians, most of them persevere in their beliefs. Because of this, many of the soldiers are converting. Also, many of them are defecting to Constantine's area to avoid harming the Christians."

Galerius responded, "Don't lie to me!"

His advisor challenged Galerius, "Perhaps it is time to change our policy. The persecution is harming the empire, isn't it time to stop?"

Galerius screamed, "There is no turning back! If we hear of anyone showing any weakness toward the Christians, they must be killed right away! We are going to win this war and there is no turning back!"

"But sir, it's not working. The persecution is having the opposite effect," said the advisor, knowing that he was taking his chances by arguing with the emperor.

"Leave at once!" yelled Galerius.

The advisor thought that he would be killed. He was amazed that he survived his meeting. Soon after, he fled to Constantine's region.

CHAPTER 19

MONTH TEN: "ONE FLOCK"

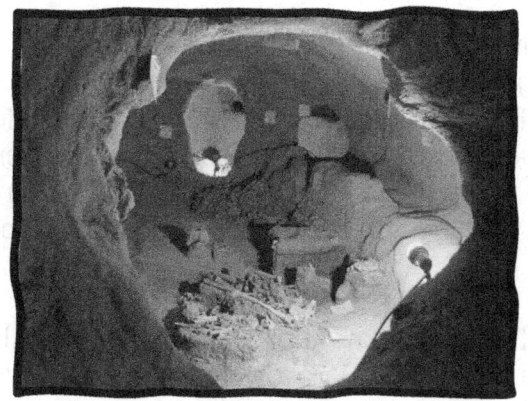
Underground City Apartment, Meyer, CC

Daniel began their meeting by saying, "This is our final sermon on unity! I tell you; it is a different world down here compared to when we started our teaching!"

He turned to the crowd and asked, "Am I right?"

Everybody nodded and cheered with enthusiasm.

He continued, "I'm going to read from John's Gospel:

> "I have other sheep that are not of this sheep pen. I must bring them also. They will listen to my voice. There will be one flock and one shepherd."
>
> -John 10:16

"If someone is truly listening to God's voice, he will lead the believers around him into unity. Jesus' voice is calling us into unity. Look! Jesus says, 'They will listen to my voice!' Then he says, 'there will be one flock and one shepherd' How did we not see this before the persecution? Clearly, He is calling us into unity!

"Christians put their traditions above the scriptures. They tend to exalt their dogma above the will of God. The word of God unites us together. The devil knows this. Our endless disputes about doctrine should never tear us apart because the scriptures teach unity! When a believer subverts his desire for power and pleasure to the word of God, he can be used by God and will bring believers together.

"The attitude that proclaims that everybody must change for you and follow your traditions is a divisive attitude. We must follow Jesus. We must listen to Jesus' voice as he guides us into relationship with one another!

"We are all children of God. It means that we are all one family as we all stand together under Christ!

"Let's listen to the shepherd and be one! Let's come together, holding each other through this cold dark night. We will get through this, but only through the warmth we experience when we are close to each other!"

Daniel paused, "Let's proclaim our unity right now as loud as we can to God and to one another! Let's proclaim that we are one! Let's get arm in arm and yell as loud as we can, 'We are one!' Are you ready?"

Everyone followed Daniel's instructions and locked arms.

"Say, we are one!"

The crowd proclaimed, "We are one."

Daniel said, "That will not do! Come on! Let us give it our all!"

"We are one!" yelled the crowd loudly as they laughed and smiled at one another.

Daniel looked around as he nodded his head in agreement and then said, "Markos is here. He is a new recruit to the City of Refuge, and he has a powerful story. When he shared it with me, I told him he had to proclaim what God had done for him. Markos, come forward."

Markos was 20 years old and was overjoyed to speak. He leaped up to the front and said, "Thank you Daniel. I was raised in Cappadocia, and I came to the Lord just a couple of years ago. I was recently sharing Jesus with my younger brother and unfortunately, he did not want anything to do with Christ. A brief time later, he fell in love with a girl from a wealthy family. My brother was informed by the girl's father that he had to be the heir of my parents' estate to marry her. I was the first born and the heir. Therefore, my brother went to the authorities and reported to them that I was a Christian. I was jailed for two weeks when my parents mysteriously died.

"As I sat in the cell and found out about my parents. God revealed himself to me and comforted me. It was then that I decided, I was willing to die for Christ!

"Later the Roman guards tried to convince me that I should worship Galerius and deny Jesus. I told them that I was a recent convert. As they put me on the stretching rack and began to tighten the mechanism, one of the Roman guards started whipping me senselessly. The man controlling the full process told the torturer to go tighter and tighter. I'm young and I don't want to die, but I told the torturer that I would die for Christ.

"Somebody entered the area and it's my understanding that he was a senior official. He called everyone out of the room, telling them that they had the wrong guy. After everyone left, he became emotional and said, 'I'm sick of seeing people die. Leave right now! Hurry!'

"I said, are you serious?

"He said, 'Yes, I'm going to let you go!'

"He proceeded to undo the ropes, as tears flowed from both of us. He led me out of the building in chains and then secretly released me. He told me to get out of town and hide. He said that he was a new Christian and was planning to flee to Constantine's area. A lot of Christians are going there."

Everybody clapped and began to get excited.

Markos said, "God is going to break through. Don't give up!"

A few weeks later, several men from a church in Egypt arrived at the City of Refuge. These men believed that Christians should not eat meat. They caused controversy by telling people that eating meat was not acceptable to God. They spoke to the new believers, saying, "Anyone eating animals becomes a mobile cemetery of rotting flesh!" This scared and confused many of the people and so they talked to Daniel.

Daniel met with Nicolas and discussed the ideas being spread by the men. Nicolas remembered a passage in the book of Romans that discussed this specific issue. It said:

> 'As for the one who is weak in the faith, welcome him, but not to quarrel over opinions. One person believes he may eat anything, while the weak person eats only vegetables. Let not the one who eats despise the one who

abstains and let not the one who abstains pass judgment on the one who eats, for God has welcomed him.

- Romans 14:1

They asked the men how long they were planning on staying at the City of Refuge. They said that they were going to be there for just two more weeks. They were on their way to France to escape the persecution.

Daniel said to them, "Do you believe that a person can be saved and eat meat."

The men said, "Perhaps."

"Well," said Daniel, "We will not eat any meat for the next two weeks because we want to respect all of you."

They were agreeable, but obviously frustrated.

Daniel said to them, "Please don't make eating meat an issue with people. Be considerate and we will accommodate you."

Nobody had any meat for the next two weeks and the men were faithful not to discuss or bring up the issue. Meat was in short supply, so it was no problem to abstain. When the men moved out and everything was back to normal again.

CHAPTER 20

THE TUNNEL

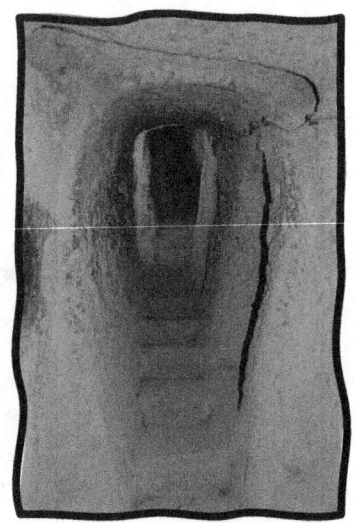

Tunnel, LW Yang, CC

308 AD

THREE YEARS AFTER BEGINNING THE TUNNEL EFFORT

FIVE YEARS INTO PERSECUTION

The population of the City of Refuge had swelled to over twenty thousand people. The men worked both day and night on the tunnel and were very weary. Many were complaining that the venture was impossible and a complete waste of time. Ozgur maintained that the tunnels would be joining each other soon, but very few people believed him.

The Tunnel

Jonathan informed Daniel of a large band of Roman soldiers attacking the entrance of New Jerusalem. Suddenly, the workers began to get much more aggressive when they heard word of the desperate situation.

At 2:02 AM on January 17th, in the year 308 AD, the tunnel workers took a short break. As they sat there, resting quietly, they heard a faint, "ding, ding, ding."

"Wait!!" said the foreman, "Do you hear that?"

"Everyone hush!" said another man.

The sound of the hammer hitting the chisel was getting louder and louder.

"Oh my!" exclaimed the foreman, "We are close!"

"Yes!" screamed another worker. Everyone started to cheer as word circulated up to The City of Refuge that the two tunnels were about to converge.

At the meeting point, rock fragments fell to the ground as the people stood back. A human figure suddenly emerged from the huge dust cloud! Other people also lunged forward!

Everyone began to grab each other in sheer joy, falling to the ground. When Daniel got word, he rejoiced. Then he quickly brought a fresh supply of sulfur through the tunnel to New Jerusalem, allowing them to continue to fend off the Romans.

A few days later, the Roman soldiers gave up and were happy to leave the area, sickened by the stench of sulfur.

309AD

YEAR SIX OF PERSECUTION

As time went on, Galerius never left his room except to go to the bathroom. His bed was huge, and yet it could barely hold him in his overweight state.

One of Galerius' top officials, a man named Hamden, asked to meet with the emperor. He entered Galerius' chamber, suppressing his reaction to the emperor's horrendous body odor.

Nervous, he bowed down at the foot of the bed and said, "Sir, I don't know if you know this, but your wife Valeria… Well, she is a Christian. Diocletian's wife, your mother-in-law, she is a Christian as well."

Galerius said to Hamden with a whisper, signaling him to come in close so the others could not hear, "So you are saying my wife and her mother are both Christians?"

"Oh, yes sir," whispered Hamden, "Most definitely."

Galerius asked in a whisper, "Have you told anyone? "

"No, I have only told you. I thought it best that I should tell you first," replied Hamden, expecting accolades and a promotion.

"Good, good," said Galerius, shaking his head in agreement, "And how did you make this discovery?"

Hamden said, "Your wife's maid sir. Your wife was trying to convert the woman as the Christians tend to do. The maid reported the situation to me."

"Well thank you so much for letting me know this," said Galerius, "I will tend to the matter immediately. You will be graciously rewarded for including me in on that little tidbit of information." He laughed as he winked at man.

"My pleasure sir," said Hamden as he smiled, "Thank you, thank you sir."

Hamden exited the room. Galerius called another top official over and said to him, "That man who just left. I can't seem to remember his name. I think it is Hamden perhaps. Yes, Hamden. He insulted me and he needs to die at once. He is spreading lies!"

Galerius wasn't prepared to kill his wife and he didn't want anyone to know that he was married to a Christian. Hamden was sent to the dungeon and immediately executed. Galerius then called for his wife. They hadn't seen each other in several years. From the beginning, their relationship was a mere formality. When she entered the room, she was smiling though terrified. Galerius ordered the guards to leave so their conversation could be private.

Galerius said, "tell me it isn't true! I hear that you and your mother are now Christian. Tell me it isn't true."

She exclaimed, "Yes and I wish that you would become one too!"

He replied, "Could you possibly say anything more ridiculous?"

"Galerius," said Valeria tenderly, "God loves all of us. The Christians are good people, and they only want to spread the message of God's love."

Galerius responded, "If you want to live, just keep that talk to yourself. I just put the man to death who informed me of your conversion. You know as well as I do, I have no problem taking your life. Don't talk to anyone about this subject! Do you hear me!"

"Why do you hate them so?" she asked, "They aren't trying to take over. They are good people just trying to survive. Why do you hate them?"

Galerius took out his bottle of wine before replying. He poured some in his cup and then took a drink.

"They are trying to take over!" said Galerius, "But, besides that, there is more to this story. You know why I hate them? I'll tell you why."

A fearful look appeared on the face of Galerius. Valeria stared at the huge globs of fat on his arms and stomach as he struggled to suddenly rise from the bed. He then closed the door to the room, making sure that nobody was able to hear their conversation.

He turned back to her and said, "The Christians cause shame and guilt! I was open to them when I was young. A man told my mother and me about the Christian God and we listened and were interested. Then the Christian dog infuriated my mother by telling her that if she became a Christian, God would change her life. She made her living by organizing orgies. He told her that her lifestyle could be improved through following Christ. (16).

"You know, I grew up with these orgies, hearing noises and seeing drunken people wandering around all night long. It scared me to death. There would be vomit all over the house the next day. I'll admit, it was disgusting, and I didn't want any part of it. However, one night they were having an orgy and a woman walked into my room. I was but eleven. She slept with me and that was my first experience. I felt guilt afterward because of what the Christians had told me about sex being wrong. After this experience, I participated in the orgies. As I grew, I realized that the Christians do nothing but cause shame and guilt! Christians only want to limit people and push their foolish brand of morality! Pleasure is power! There is power in the orgies, and I live for it! Just because I'm on top of the world doesn't mean I should allow these weaklings to intrude on my life!"

"No Galerius, you are not on top of the world," said Valeria, "There is so much more."

"No! Not for me!" said Galerius. "The Christians must be eliminated. They are only out to take over and make everyone miserable!"

She walked away as Galerius sat in his bed. He immediately called for two of his sexual slaves. After they arrived, he took a drink from a cup of wine and then stared at them. One of them was showing signs of aging. He called for his attendant and said to him, "This one displeases me, take her away at once. I never want to see her again!"

The attendant escorted her out of the room, but internally, the woman was overjoyed.

Back in Cappadocia, the population at the City of Refuge grew to over 25,000 people, all living underground together in peace and harmony. Of that number, over 4,000 had been slaves before they became residents.

The believers of New Jerusalem also began to learn and recite the unity scriptures. Everyone understood that the blessings of God flowed through their unity. They called it, 'The Unity Blessing.' Supplies continued to flow in while the gold, clothing and the scriptures flowed out.

CHAPTER 21

THE VICTORY

Galerius, Canellopoulos CC

311AD

EIGHT YEARS FROM THE START OF THE PERSECUTION

Galerius began to lose his ability to perform sexually. He became so fat that his attendants laughed behind his back as they watched him barely make it through the doorway.

The Victory

One day he went into the bathroom and sat down to move his bowels. A young attendant stood at his side, waiting to use a special sponge on the emperor's bottom. As the servant applied the sponge, Galerius experienced excruciating pain rip through his body. He then fell to the ground and was unable to get up while screaming in anguish. The attendant was terrified, thinking he would be blamed for Galerius' pain. Three soldiers rushed in to assist the emperor off the floor as the bathroom attendant was escorted to the dungeon. Suddenly, a horrific odor accompanied the emperor. All those attending to his needs could only tolerate a few minutes at a time with him.

He called for a physician and when he arrived, Galerius said, "I feel like my stomach is filled with broken shards of glass! I believe I've been poisoned. There must have been something on that sponge."

"Let's examine you," said the physician as he trembled, "You are going to be okay."

Disgusted by the odor, the physician examined Galerius and saw visible black tumors. He decided to remove them surgically. He required Galerius to drink a large quantity of wine before the procedure. After removing the tumors, the physician called for three beautiful virgins from the temple to dance before him.

When the women arrived, they were disgusted by the foul odor in the room. They tried to be seductive and flaunt their beauty, but in their repulsed state, they couldn't perform. One of them ran out of the room and vomited in the hallway. The other women exited, and Galerius heard the women talking among themselves just outside his door. He thought they were making jokes about him. Embarrassed, Galerius commanded that everyone leave.

He called for the doctor again. By now he was in greater pain as the alcohol began to wear off. When the doctor arrived, he fearfully walked to Galerius' bedside. The emperor screamed at the top of his lungs, "I'm not doing better and in fact, I'm much worse because of your foolishness!"

"Well sir," said the terrified doctor, "I have some other medicines to try. The emperor needs to drink this."

He handed Galerius a solution in a small clay bottle. The emperor grabbed the medication and threw it on the polished floor as the bottle shattered into a thousand pieces.

"Guards!" screamed Galerius as he stared at the physician, longing to see the look of terror on his face, "I want you to behead this man right now in the dungeon!" (17)

Killing always gave Galerius a quick sense of superiority and strength. Galerius delighted himself in the moment. For a second, he was given relief and distracted from his physical and emotional pain.

Two other doctors were called in to meet with him, but when they smelled the stench coming from the room, they refused to enter. Galerius could hear them outside.

He yelled at the top of his lungs, "Are you refusing to assist me? I am god and I have the power of life and death!" The guards led them away so they would not be killed.

"I am a god," yelled Galerius, "And I am the most powerful man in the entire world! Fix this now!"

Inwardly, all his attendants rejoiced with the hope that he would soon be dead. After getting word about the death of the doctor, no physician would come near him.

The Victory

A few days later, Galerius called for his wife. Her mother Priscilla happened to be visiting. The two entered the room as their nostrils were met by the horrible stench.

The emperor's body was shaking, and he was gasping for air. He said to Valeria right away, "What must I do to appease this Christian God?"

Valeria thought carefully about her words. She said, "Galerius, there is only one God and he created everything. You are just a man."

Galerius said, "Now is not the time to lecture me!"

"You can stop the persecution," Valeria said, "The Christians have no weapons but one. Amidst this war against them, the Christians pray, and the only true God listens to them. Perhaps they will pray for you and the God who created you will heal you."

"Forget this stupid talk!" said Galerius jerking and writhing in pain, "Obviously, I am not going to ask the Christians to pray for me!"

Galerius sat up from his bed for a moment and then called for his top advisor. When the man arrived, he said while struggling, "I need to declare a worldwide edict. It must go out immediately!"

The man started writing and said, "Go ahead sir."

"It is to be called The Edict of Toleration," said Galerius as he struggled to speak his words. He then looked at Valeria and her mother and said, "Perhaps this will satisfy your God."

Galerius worked with the advisor to compose the edict. After it was completed, he used his signet ring to officiate the document. The next day, he began to cough uncontrollably with saliva dripping down his face, cursing with his last gasps of air, his body began to shake violently and then stopped suddenly. He lay there on his back with his eyes wide open.

His attendants checked his breathing.

"He's dead!" said the attendant.

All the soldiers and attendants applauded and cheered, jumping for joy as word spread throughout the palace. Everyone was rejoicing.

Word quickly spread throughout the Roman Empire about Galerius' death as the edict was placed on public buildings. Believers rejoiced when they received word but were still secretive and afraid. Many Christian slaves were released, as many prisoners awaiting execution also were set free.

Jonathan arrived late at night at the City of Refuge. Daniel and his men opened the huge stone door. Food was in short supply and so Daniel was anxious to meet with Jonathan. When they approached each other, Daniel asked, "Where are the supplies?"

"I have bad news," said Jonathan, "But then I'm also going to give you good news so don't be upset."

"Okay," said Daniel.

"I have not brought you any food," said Jonathan.

Daniel was outraged. "Why? You know we've got 25,000 people living here and we do not have food!"

"Daniel," said Jonathan with a secure calm voice, "Here is the good news," he paused and waited for Daniel to look him in the eye. "Galerius is dead and just before he died, he released this edict proclaiming that the persecution is over!"

He handed Daniel a parchment.

"What?" asked Daniel.

"Read it," said Jonathan.

Daniel looked at the paper and checked the seal to see if it was official. He carefully read the words:

THE EDICT OF TOLERATION
(shortened)

We had desired to bring into harmony the ancient laws of the Romans, and to provide that even the Christians, who had left the religion of their fathers should come back to reason; since, indeed, the Christians themselves, had fallen into such a folly that they would not obey the rules of the ancients.

By their own will and pleasure, they would make their own laws which they had to observe and would gather in various places in congregations. Finally, when our law had been enforced to the effect that they should conform, many were subdued by the fear of danger, many suffered death. Most of them persevered in their determination, and we saw that they neither paid the reverence and awe due to the gods.

In view of our habit by which we grant freedom to all, we thought that we ought to grant permission also to these, so that they may

again be Christians, provided they do nothing contrary to good order.

Wherefore, we ask this of them, that they ought to pray to their God for our safety, for that of the republic, and for their own, that the republic may continue uninjured on every side, and that they may be able to live securely in their homes.

This edict is published at Nicaea, in the month of May.

"It can't be!" said Daniel as tears gushed out of his eyes. He looked up at Jonathan.

"Daniel, it's true!" said Jonathan, "In town, even the Roman soldiers are celebrating in the streets. The tyrant is dead, and the persecution is over! Licinus, the brother-in-law of Constantine, has taken over and word is out that he is a Christian!"

Daniel sprang to his feet and screamed with joy. He ran back into The City of Refuge and called for an emergency meeting. They all stopped their work and came to the large worship room.

Looking at Anasia among the crowd, he said jubilantly, "Everyone, be quiet! Jonathan just gave me the report that he will not be bringing us grain and I don't care! Why don't I care you ask? Galerius is dead and the persecution is officially over!"

"What?" echoed several people.

"Galerius is dead, and the persecution is over!" proclaimed Daniel.

Everyone was silent.

The Victory

Daniel said with the document held over his head, "Before Galerius died, he released The Edict of Toleration! That is what I am holding here in my hand!" He proceeded to read the words to everyone as many fell to the ground in shock and joyful disbelief.

After finishing, he added, "With his parting words, Galerius has asked us to pray for the Roman Empire! Can you believe it! You better believe that we are going to pray! We will pray until they completely abandon their gods and serve the only true God!"

Ozgur ran over to Daniel and grabbed the document. After giving it a look, he fell to the ground and was shaking with emotion. Others took turns grabbing it and reading it huddled in a circle, touching the seal. It all just seemed too good to be true.

After a period of commotion Daniel said, "Everyone, quiet down! We are going to have the biggest worship time we've ever had right now! It's time to celebrate! However, we need to be careful and test the waters, but from what I hear, they are jumping for joy all over Cappadocia!" Let's lift our hands right now and praise the Lord! He has answered our prayers!"

They began to sing a song and tearfully worship God with all their hearts.

After singing, Daniel said to the crowd, "Hey everyone, we are going to have a huge party to celebrate!"

He gave Jonathan the gold that Gilley had hidden and told him to buy lambs and special bread for everyone.

Jonathan later returned with the lambs and other Cappadocian delicacies such as figs and special mint tea. They feasted from morning to night.

Afterwards, Daniel got up and said, "Let's not forget what we have learned here! I have some money that we will be distributing so that everybody has something, but first we are going to pray."

With these words everybody reflected in silence on the lessons of eight long years.

Daniel continued, "Please continue to keep the city a secret, we don't know if we are going to have to come back!"

They prayed for everyone and then began to release a few people at a time. Daniel walked up to the two men from the Library of Caesarea Maritima. He asked them what they wanted to do.

They said, "Daniel, this is the safest place for us to keep making copies of the scriptures. Until we are 100 percent sure that the writings are safe, we would rather stay here. Daza may still be in power in Israel. Let's wait.

Daniel said, "We will continue to provide for you and support you any way we can."

The men who were tattooed slaves wanted to remain in the city. They would be apprehended, tortured, and killed if they were seen in public. Daniel chose to allow them to stay underground and live as a community. Most of them had learned to read and write and were now copying the scriptures. They were able to provide for their needs with the gold and other minerals they discovered down below.

They released thousands of people just a couple of days before Daniel and Anasia left the City of Refuge. As he stood outside, there was a different feeling in the air. He wasn't experiencing the fear that he had known for so long.

The Victory

He and Ansasia held hands as they made the walk into town with Ozgur and Calista. It was the most amazing moment of their lives. They laughed and rejoiced the whole way.

When they reached the center of town, there was a huge group of people celebrating with music and food. The four of them joined in the festivities.

Daniel eventually discovered that Cyprian the tax collector had moved away from the area, and that his debt had been cleared.

Most of the Christians stayed with relatives and friends because a large percentage of them had lost their property.

The Christians of Cappadocia continued to meet, read the scriptures, and pray daily in people's homes. They still could not retrieve their churches and houses.

Word reached them that Daza turned against The Edict of Toleration and was persecuting the Christians in his domain. He continued to secretly conspire with Maxentius as the two ramped up their plans to conquer and rule the Empire.

CHAPTER 22

THE RISE OF CONSTANTINE

Constantine, Musei Capitolini CC

312AD

When Constantine received the news about Galerius' death and that Maxentius' had partnered with Daza, he decided to attack Rome. Seizing the city was no easy task and his advisors insisted that his plans were absurd.

Despite huge challenges, Constantine traveled down from France to Italy with 100,000 of his best men, standing victorious against several smaller armies along the way. Many of the members of his army were Christians that had traveled to his region from heavily persecuted areas.

The residents of each city he conquered rejoiced with a huge celebration, overjoyed to sit under his leadership.

Christians all over the world were praying for victory for Constantine. Constantine had never persecuted any of the believers in his region, although it was uncertain where he stood with Christianity.

As Constantine's army approached Rome, Maxentius did what he had done previously when he was attacked by Severus and Galerius. He sent beautiful women into the camp of Constantine's army, offering luxuries and houses to convince them that they should defect.

Before the battle, Constantine told all his soldiers to paint a Christian symbol on their shields. The Christians in his military were excited and impassioned at this command. They figured Constantine must be a strong believer, and so they persuaded everyone to ignore the beautiful seducers and fight for Constantine. Nobody defected as they marched to attack. (Author's Note: It has been recorded in history that Constantine saw a 'Chi Rho' in the sky and heard the words, 'By this symbol you shall conquer.' Please read the 'Final Thoughts' section for more information).

Maxentius received reports of Constantine's army and asked the Roman Oracle what he should do. The Oracle stated that on 'October 28th, an enemy of Rome will perish.' Maxentius interpreted this to mean that he should fight Constantine on that exact day.

Word was communicated to Constantine about the prophecy. Constantine rejoiced, knowing that Maxentius was compelled to fight him on October 28th. He ordered his men to pull a far distance away from the main bridge that led into Rome, figuring that Maxentius would pursue his army to beat the clock and fight on that exact day.

Constantine watched joyfully from a distance as Maxentius and thousands of his troops began to leave the safety of Rome and cross the narrow short bridge, just as he had hoped. The walls and towers of Rome were no longer a factor, he could fight in the open. Constantine ordered some of his men to cross the river down the way and destroy the bridge from the opposite side.

Constantine was vastly outnumbered, but he and his men possessed a strong confidence. When the battle erupted and the two sides clashed, immediately, the troops of Maxentius suffered huge losses. His men began to desperately retreat but discovered that the end of the bridge had been destroyed. The river's pure waters turned beet red as man and horse fell off from the bridge and into the water. Constantine was able to obliterate the troops of Maxentius quickly and completely.

After the battle was finished, one of Constantine's men reported that he had seen Maxentius fall into the water. They searched through the frigid waters and retrieved the body of Maxentius.

The day after the conflict, Constantine entered Rome in his chariot and celebrated his victory. He held the head of Maxentius high in the air as the people lined the streets cheering (19). The people of Rome gladly accepted Constantine as their new leader.

Daniel and the believers of Cappadocia once again had reason to rejoice when they heard word of Constantine's victory. Their faith in God's power to transform the world increased to new heights.

313AD

TWO YEARS AFTER THE RELEASE OF THE EDICT OF TOLERATION

Helena arrived at Constantine's palace in Rome and pleaded with her son regarding the rights of the Christians. She insisted that he restore all their property.

Constantine set up a meeting in Milan, Italy to draft a new edict. It was the first time in history that the Roman Empire legalized any other religion besides the Roman religion. It also allowed Christians the right to take back the property that was taken from them during the persecution.

While working with the leader of the church of Milan to pen the document, the man asked Constantine, "With all that you are doing to help the Christians, surely you must want to convert and be baptized?"

Constantine refused. The church leader was greatly perplexed. Nobody knew for sure where Constantine stood, but they were thankful that he was not persecuting the Christians. They named the new treaty, 'The Treaty of Milan.'

Daniel was in town when Cappadocia received the new edict. The Christians held a huge gathering and read the document at the center of town to a joyous crowd. It was as exciting as when they received 'The Edict of Toleration.' Now there were strong leaders making a stand for freedom. Everyone was in tear and amazed at God's faithfulness to answer their prayers.

The believers were able to receive back their churches and their homes, except for Daniel. He and his wife lived with friends. Gilley had sold their house right after taking possession and they had no recourse to get it back.

Meanwhile in the area to the south of Cappadocia where Daza was the emperor, the tyrant was able to maintain his reign over the people. He knew that his only hope was to attack and defeat Constantine. He quickly assembled his army, and to the horror of the believers of Cappadocia, he took over their entire area. The

Christians retreated to the City of Refuge, having stockpiled the storerooms with supplies. Daniel and his friends turned their fears into prayers. Their confidence was high, despite Daza's advances.

Daza had twice the number of troops compared to the Roman regiment in Greece. Daza continued to make his way north. When the two forces clashed in an area close to Cappadocia, Daza quickly saw his numbers dwindling and defeat on the horizon.

He escaped the battlefield and disguised himself in civilian clothes. Pretending to be a commoner, he went into the market area to buy some wine, shaken by the battle and his losses. A merchant recognized him as multitudes of people began to chase him down. He turned a corner and pulled out a small vial of poison. Drinking it as fast as he could, he died as the crowd carried him through the streets.

Soon afterward, a victory arch was built for Constantine in Rome. At the unveiling ceremony, a huge tarp was pulled away as the images on the arch were revealed. Constantine was not present for the ceremony, but the Christians were infuriated when they saw Christian icons mixed with the sun god and other pagan imagery. Many believers were terrified, sensing that the teachings of Christ would be maligned by the Roman gods. Others said, "This proves that the emperor only manipulates for power, but at least he is not persecuting us."

Back in Cappadocia, the people were getting reacclimated to normal life. Daniel used all the money from the gold to provide for the slaves and the copies being made at the City of Refuge. Sadly, there was no permanent house for Daniel and Anasia.

One day, the believers of Cappadocia decided to hold a huge celebration in honor of the couple, expressing appreciation for their help during the persecution.

At the start of the event, Nicolas had all the people gather as he jumped in front of the crowd. He said to Daniel and Anasia, "You gave everything for us during those difficult years, and so it is only right that we do something really special for you!"

Nicolas pointed to a cave-house that was right across the street from where they were meeting. He said, "You see that house over there, the one with lots of windows and the funny looking hat? That is your new house!"

Cappadocian Cave House CC

Anasia laughed hysterically when she saw the house. She ran across the street and blazed through the front door. Daniel walked over and met her in the upper room.

Anasia said to Daniel, "It's the strangest house I've ever seen, but after living underground for eight years, you have to love it!"

They held each other as they looked at the crowd out the window with everyone cheering. They soon went downstairs into the living room to meet Ozgur and Calista.

"Was this your design Ozgur?" asked Daniel.

"You bet!" said Ozgur. "Let's just say we had some fun with it!"

"It makes me laugh, but you know what, we love it!" said Daniel as he looked into the blue eyes of Anasia. The couple was overjoyed because the people created the house out of gratitude. They liked it much more than the cave house that Gilley had taken.

People traveled from all over Cappadocia to see the house because of the unique design. Their cave opened the door for them to share the Gospel with all the onlookers.

The Christians of Cappadocia continued to be united. They helped each other get reestablished with homes and businesses. Everyone flourished under the united government of Constantine.

They also took advantage of the opportunity to share Jesus without fear. Many people came to believe, including Roman soldiers. They were touched by the steadfast faith of the believers during the persecution.

Daniel and Anasia were able to obtain a loan to buy the Inn that was taken away from them by Gilley. Their business was highly successful as they created a warm environment for travelers, sharing the gospel with their employees and guests.

Ozgur and Calista bought a house right next to Daniel and Anasia. Everything changed very quickly. It all seemed like a dream to the Christians of Cappadocia. Every Sunday when they gathered, there was incredible appreciation. They continued to enjoy meeting for dinner like a big happy family.

To the awe of the Christians, many Roman temples were suddenly being converted to churches.

One day Marcus from Thessaloniki, the man that had brought the scriptures to his city, arrived in Cappadocia to make a wonderful announcement. He proclaimed that Galerius' temple was being converted into a church! All the believers were ecstatic! Nobody ever could have imagined that their prayers could be answered so quickly.

The two men from the Library of Caesarea met with Daniel one day and said, "It is time for us to go back."

Daniel was happy. "Mission accomplished!" he exclaimed as he hugged the brothers. The writings were carefully sent back to Caesarea in Israel and the library was reestablished as a central hub for the scriptures to be copied and distributed throughout the world.

The number of runaway Christian slaves living down below in The City of Refuge continued to grow. Constantine stopped the practice of branding of the faces of the slaves, but the slaves were still horribly mistreated. Daniel let them stay in the city and continued to help provide for their needs. He stayed true to his word to offer the City of Refuge as a sacrifice to the Lord. All the gold that was mined from the city was used to provide for their needs.

325AD

About 14 years after the persecution ended, Nicolas went to Daniel's house and told him about a meeting that was going to take place in Nicaea.

He said, "Daniel, for the first time since the days of the early church, Christians from all over the world are going to come together as one! I would like you and Ozgur to join me in Nicaea for an amazing meeting. It is the fulfillment of Jesus' prayer for unity!"

Daniel and Ozgur enthusiastically agreed.

While they were traveling, they discussed the irony of the situation. They were about to embark on a historic meeting in Nicaea, the same city that was the starting point of the persecution. They reflected over the incredible transformation that happened over a brief time, marveling at the faithfulness of God to answer their prayers and lead them to victory.

As the meeting began, everyone sang a hymn in perfect unison. Then they discussed the issues that were causing division. To help prevent division in the future, they decided to compose a simple statement that clearly defined what it meant to be a Christian. After much discussion, they named it, 'The Nicene Creed.' (20)

When Daniel returned home, he was absolutely buzzing with enthusiasm as he relayed his experience to Anasia.

The couple's inn expanded as all the Christians of Cappadocia continued to prosper and grow in unity.

Daniel and Anasia never had their own children, but they always had a huge happy family.

ADDITIONAL PICTURES:

Constantine Arch, WC, CC

The Milvian Bridge, CC

Arch of Constantine, NikonZ7II, CC

EXTRAS

THE UNITY SCRIPTURES

John 17:20-22

"I do not ask on behalf of these alone, but for those also who believe in Me through their word; that they may all be one; even as You, Father, are in Me and I in You, that they also may be in Us, so that the world may believe that You sent Me."

John 17:22-23

"The glory which You have given Me I have given to them, that they may be one, just as We are one; I in them and You in Me, that they may be perfected in unity, so that the world may know that You sent Me, and loved them, even as You have loved Me."

1 Corinthians 12:12

"Just as a body, though one, has many parts, but all its many parts forms one body, so it is with Christ. We were baptized by one Holy Spirit into one body. It didn't matter whether we were Jews or Greeks, slaves, or free people. We were all given the same Spirit to drink."

Ephesians 4:2

"Be completely humble and gentle; be patient, bearing with one another in love. Make every effort to keep the unity of the Spirit through the bond of peace. There is one body and one Spirit, just as you were called to one hope when you were called; one Lord, one faith, one baptism; one God and Father of all, who is over all and through all and in all."

Romans 15:5

"May the God who gives endurance and encouragement give you the same attitude of mind toward each other that Christ Jesus had, so that with one mind and one voice you may glorify the God and Father of our Lord Jesus Christ. Accept one another, then, just as Christ accepted you, to bring praise to God."

Psalm 133:1-3

"How good and pleasant it is when God's people live together in unity. It is like precious oil poured on the head. Running down on the beard. Running down on Aaron's beard. Down on the color of his robe. It is like the dew of Harmon. We're falling Mount Zion. For there, the Lord bestows His blessing, even life evermore."

1 Corinthians 1:10

"I appeal to you, brothers, in the name of our Lord Jesus Christ, that all of you agree with one another so that there may be no divisions among you and that you may be perfectly united in mind and thought."

2 Corinthians 13:11

"Be perfect, be of good comfort, be of one mind, live in peace; and the God of love and peace shall be with you."

Matthew 5:24

"Therefore, if you are offering your gift at the altar and there remember that your brother or sister has something against you, leave your gift there in front of the altar. First go and be reconciled to them; then come and offer your gift."

John 10:16

"I have other sheep that are not of this sheep pen. I must bring them also. They will listen to my voice. There will be one flock and one shepherd."

THE EDICT OF MILAN
Created in Milan, Italy in 313

"Now, we, Constantine and Licinus, emperors, met at Milan in conference concerning the welfare and security of the realm, we decided that of the things that are of profit to all mankind, the worship of God ought rightly to be our first and chiefest care, and that it was the right that Christians and all others should have freedom to follow the kind of religion they favored; so that the God who dwells in heaven might be propitious to us and all under our rule.

We therefore announce that, notwithstanding any provisions concerning the Christians in our former instruction all who choose that religion are to be permitted to continue therein, without any let or hindrance, and are not in any way troubled or molested.

Moreover, concerning the Christians, we before gave orders with respect to the places set apart for their worship. It is now our pleasure that all who have bought such places should restore them to the Christians, without any demand for payment. (Owners could apply to the state for compensation).

You are to use your utmost diligence in carrying out these orders on behalf of the Christians... So shall that divine favor which we have already enjoyed in affairs of the greatest moment, continue to grant us success, and thus secure the happiness of the realm.

NICENE CREED

Created in Nicaea in 325AD.

We believe in one God, the Father Almighty, the maker of heaven and earth, of things visible and invisible. And in one Lord Jesus Christ, the Son of God, the begotten of God the Father, the Only begotten, that is of the essence of the Father.

God of God, Light of Light, true God of true God, begotten and not made; of the very same nature of the Father, by Whom all things came into being, in heaven and on earth, visible and invisible.

Who for us humanity and for our salvation came down from heaven, was incarnate, was made human, was born perfectly of the holy virgin Mary by the Holy Spirit. By whom he took body, soul, and mind, and everything that is in man, truly and not in semblance.

He suffered, was crucified, was buried, rose again on the third day, ascended into heaven with the same body, and sat at the right hand of the Father. He is to come with the same body and with the glory of the Father, to judge the living and the dead; of his kingdom there is no end.

We believe in the Holy Spirit in the uncreated and the perfect; Who spoke through the Law, prophets, and Gospels; Who came down upon the Jordon, preached through the apostles, and lived in the saints.

We believe in One, Universal, Apostolic and (Holy) Church; In one baptism in repentance, for the remission, and forgiveness of sins; and in the resurrection of the dead, in the everlasting judgement of souls and bodies and the Kingdom of Heaven and in everlasting life.

ANCIENT TUNNELS

The ancients created many amazing tunnels. The most common technique was to work from both sides and then meet in the middle using a vast array of engineering techniques.

TUNNEL EUPALINOS - 6TH CENTURY BC

Tunnel of Eupalinos, Dorieo21, CC

In the 1800s, archeologists discovered an ancient map that led to the discovery of a long tunnel in Greece called the Tunnel of Eupalinos, built in the 6th century BC. The documents illustrated in detail the techniques employed to create a mile long tunnel that met in the middle of a large mountain.

SILOAM TUNNEL - 8TH CENTURY BC

Siloam Tunnel, Tamar Havardeni CC

Under Jerusalem in Israel is a tunnel built through the bedrock by King Hezekiah. The Bible mentions the tunnel in three separate places, but Second Kings gives the best description of the tunnel:

> "As for the other events of Hezekiah's reign, all his achievements and how he made the pool and the tunnel by which he brought water into the tunnel by which he brought water into the city, are they not written in the book of the annals of the kings of Judah?"
>
> **2nd Kings 20:20**

The tunnel was discovered in the early 1800s by Edward Robinson, an American archeologist. In 1880, a young boy was traveling through the tunnel when he found a plaque on the wall. It was written in ancient Hebrew and proclaimed that the spot of the plaque was the exact point where two teams met when constructing the tunnel. It describes the celebration that occurred when the two sides heard the picks at work.

Siloam Inscription, Wikikati CC

".... the tunnel...and this is the story of the tunnel while the axes were against each other and while three cubits were left to cut... the voices of a man... called to his counterpart (for) there was Zada in the rock, on the right... and on the day of the tunnel (being finished) the stonecutter struck each man towards his counterpart, ax against ax and flowed water from the source to the pool for 1200 cubits and 100 cubits was the height over the head of the stonecutters..."

Lidzbarski, Handbuch der Nordsemitischen Epigraphik, p. 439.

The five-mile tunnel connecting two cities in Cappadocia is one of the longest tunnels created in the ancient world (before 600AD).

FINAL THOUGHTS

Right after the Great Persecution period ended, many important Church leaders emerged from Cappadocia. These men helped forge concepts regarding the trinity while helping maintain unity within the church. They became known as the "Cappadocian Fathers."

The Cappadocian Fathers are Basil the Great, Gregory of Nyssa and Gregory of Naianzus.

After the rise of Constantine, the Library of Caesarea Maritima was reestablished as a place for the scriptures to be recopied. Jerome, who put together the first modern Bible (Latin Vulgate), extensively used the library. Unfortunately, in the 7th century, the entire treasury of writings was destroyed by invading Muslim forces.

Constantine was a mysterious man. On a family vacation to Rome in 326AD, he had his faithful son Crispus killed and his second wife tortured to death in a hot bath. Historians have long guessed as to the reasons, but Constantine destroyed all the records.

From observing his behavior through history, I personally believe that he was an opportunist and manipulated people for power. One of the greatest controversies in history is his claim to have seen a Christian symbol known as the Chi Rho (pronounced ki-ro) in the sky. Before his great battle on the Melvian bridge outside of Rome, he reports seeing the "Chi Rho" and hearing the saying, "By this symbol you shall conquer." Supposedly, he had all his soldiers paint the Chi Rho on their shields before the battle. The Chi Rho was a popular Christian symbol of the early church.

Ancient Chi Rho, Dnalor CC

Did he see the symbol in a vision or was he trying to persuade the Christians in his military to fight with more ferocity? The armies of Severus and Galerius were offered luxuries and succumbed to temptation. Did he expect the same tactic from Maxentius? Did he produce this story so the Christians would fight with all their hearts? Many Christians had defected to his area.

Can a Christian kill his son and have his wife tortured to death? Would a Christian ever do such a thing?

The answer is clearly no. King David weeps over his son when he dies. Certainly, being an emperor was a challenging position with everyone wanting their power. His situation reveals his fears, but killing your son and wife?

Before he killed his wife, she uncovered a plot by her own father, Maximian, to have Constantine killed. Maximian was killed as a result as she had proved herself loyal.

However, this is a controversial question and only God knows the answer.

No doubt, he did a lot of good. As for slavery, the Roman Empire continued to have slaves under Constantine, but he demanded that they stop branding slaves on their faces. The Romans continued to fight wars and enslave the opposing army.

Under Constantine, the world was better for everyone. However, was he a Christian leader? Perhaps he only became a Christian before his death. He refused baptism up until two days before his death in 337AD.

Constantine, in the classic Roman style of leadership, made the Jews his enemy. He pinned the death of Christ on the Jews to divert blame away from the Roman Empire. It's always easy to attack the weak to appear strong.

Unfortunately, it didn't take long before the Christians of the fourth century began persecuting the Jews. In 388AD, from the very city from which The Edict of Milan was released, the Bishop of Milan sanctioned the burning of a synagogue.

Let us never forget the sufferings of past generations and may we always seek to lead everybody to Christ, especially the Jews. They carry a blessing and have blessed us with the scriptures. Jesus rejoiced when a son of Abraham repented. The book of Romans declares that the 'gifts and callings of God are irrevocable.' (Romans 11:29)

Visiting Cappadocia

Today, Cappadocia is becoming a popular tourist destination. People are enchanted by the cave houses and unusual rock formations.

Turkey was where the first century church took root outside of Israel, but today Turkey is dominated by Islam. This country of 74 million people has the second lowest percentage of Christians on the planet. Only Yemen has a lower Christian population.

The devil never gives up. The Christians that built the underground cities were able to withstand some of the harshest times in history. And yet today, this area is spiritually barren of Christian believers.

A united church can reach places like Turkey with the Gospel. It is time to become the Spotless Bride, one with the Father and one with each other.

Jesus said:

> "He who has my commandments and keeps them is the one who loves me and will be loved by my Father, and I will love him and disclose Myself to him."
>
> -John 14:20

As we maintain unity, Jesus will disclose himself to us more and more.

What was Jesus' new commandment? That we love one another.

Let's become the generation that gets it right. Let's say "YES!" to unity. Let's become passionate about becoming 'one', just as Jesus was passionate in demonstrating his love to us.

"I have other sheep that are not of this sheep pen. I must bring them also. They will listen to my voice. There will be one flock and one shepherd."
-John 10:16

Let's listen to the good shepherd's voice and become one flock. Can we put aside our differences and desires for power? Can we fulfill the calling?

The answer is yes. We can be the generation that gets it right!

NOTES

1. Potter, The Roman Empire at Bay, p. 293.

2. Eusebius, *Vita Constantine* 2.50. Davies (80 n.75) believes that this should be re-written as "the *profane* on earth" also Barnes, *Constantine, and Eusebius*, 21; Elliott, 35–36; 381; Lane Fox, 595; Liebeschuetz, 235–52, 246–48; Odahl, 67; Potter, 338 Description of Diocletian. Dictionary of Christian Biography and Literature to the End of the Sixth Century AD, Henry Wace, Boston, Little Brown Company, 1911 P255 (Authors Note: Galerius' triumph over the Persians happened in 299 and the discussion regarding the persecution occurred in 302. For the sake of the story, I combined the two events.

3. I, 7-13 Livy, Ab Urbe Condita 1, 7-13.

4. Eusebius: Hist. Ecc., Book VIII, ch. 2, ch.6 at end, and De Mart. Palest. ch- 3, ch. 4, and ch. 9.

5. Dictionary of Christian Biography and Literature to the End of the Sixth Century AD, Henry Wace, Boston, Little Brown Company, 1911 Page 626.

6. Some writings claim that Priscilla offered prayers at the Festival of Termination, however the sources cannot be verified. **6.5 Barnes, Constantine, and Eusebius, 22; Clarke, 650; Odahl, 67–69; Potter, 337.**

7. Dictionary of Christian Biography and Literature to the End of the Sixth Century AD, Henry Wace, Boston, Little Brown Company, 1911 Page 626.

8. Edict Against the Christians, Eusebius, Church History 8.24.

9. Eusebius, De Martyribus Palestinae 2 Note: This story includes Galerius cutting out someone's tongue and mentions that this was Galerius' custom.

10. Eusebius of Ceasarea, "Ecclesiastical History," VII.xxxii.25 Lactantius, *De Mortibus Persecutorum* 13.2 and Eusebius, *Historia Ecclesiastica* 8.5.1; Barnes, *Constantine, and Eusebius*, 22; Corcoran, *Empire*, 179; Williams, 176. The quotation is from Lactantius, and the translation by Williams. (Note: The name and location along with timing was changed for the sake of the story. The first person to be martyred was in Nicomedia).

11. Eusebius, De Martyribus Palestinae 3.1; Barnes, Constantine, and Eusebius, 24; Liebeschuetz, 249–50; de Ste Croix, "Aspects", 77.

12. When the people of Rome heard that it was requested that they pay taxes, riots occurred. Maxentius was married to Galerius' daughter and yet Galerius rejected him as emperor.

13. Galerius raping and pillaging after the battle in Rome. Constantine: Dynasty, Religion and Power in the Later Roman Empire, Timothy Barnes, 2013 After his troops continued to defect, he begged them to stay with him, and then he allowed them to rape and pillage throughout Italy returning home.

14. Quote from Diocletian about greed. Aurelius Victor, Liber de Caesaribus 39.6.

15. Regarding where Galerius gained his hatred toward the Christians: The Martyrs, De Chateubriand, Bariel De Gonet, Paris, 1847 "The mother of this Caesar, a woman of a gross and superstitious mind, was accustomed in the her native hamlet to offer sacrifices to her mountain divinities, Indignant that the disciples of the Gospel refused to share in her idolatries, she inspired her son with the aversion that she felt toward the faithful." The author also goes into great detail about Galerius personal love for brutal orgies.

16. Eusebius. 352-356 Describes how Galerius became fat. Goes into detail regarding his death. 1. Mahan, Milo. P. 348. *History of the Church,* New York: Pott, Young and Company, 1878 "In the East, Galerius giving himself up to dissolute living, fell a prey to that horrible loathsome disease, which is famous for having quelled the pride of two other distinguished persecutors, Herod the Great and Arram II of Spain. He was almost literally eaten up of worms." A tumor, badly healed, festered into spreading sore, which became a nest of innumerable vermin and filled the whole Palace at Nicomedia with its pestilential effluvia. In vain Apollo was applied for relief. Nurses and physicians could approach the sick man only at the peril of their lives. Under the torture of this fearful plague, his body visibly corrupting from day to day, but mind still struggling with natural feelings of remorse, he at length put forth an edict of toleration, remarkable for its apologetic and almost penitent tone."

17. Edict of Toleration, Lactantius, De Mort. Pers. ch. 34, 35. Opera, ed. O. F. Fritzsche, II, P. 273. (Bibl. Patt. Ecc. Lat. XI, Leipzig, 1844,

18. Battle with Maxentius, Lactantius, 44.5–9.

19. The Nicaean Creed, Translated from the Armenian version. The Christianity of Constantine the Great, The Catholic Historic Review, Pohlsander, P. 19 Vol. 84 No. 3, July 1998.

ABOUT THE AUTHOR

Edward Feuer was raised in Southern California and became a follower of Christ when he was 15 years old. After graduating from UCSD in San Diego, he began his work in the film industry. He was the Director of Sony Entertainment's first DVD, a project entitled "Odyssey to the Mind's Eye". Further on in his career, he helped to produce a drug prevention series for the public schools entitled, "A Natural High." The series continues to be one of the top drug prevention programs in the country. He went on to produce and direct a successful Christian surf film entitled, 'Changes.'

His last project featured Arab Muslims that had come to Christ entitled, "The Sun Rises." The film was aired throughout the Arab world and was distributed through underground churches where persecution is strong.

The Underground City of Cappadocia is his first novel.

Made in United States
Orlando, FL
25 May 2025